MW00877135

STAR SPANGLED SHARIAH

The Rise of America's First

Muslim Brotherhood Party

CIVILIZATION JIHAD READER SERIES

Volume 5

ISBN-13: 978-1517059415

ISBN-10: 1517059410

Copyright © 2015, All rights reserved.

Star Spangled Shariah: The Rise of America's First Muslim Brotherhood Party
is published in the United States by the Center for Security Policy Press,
a division of the Center for Security Policy.

September 1, 2015

THE CENTER FOR SECURITY POLICY
1901 Pennsylvania Avenue, Suite 201 Washington, DC 20006
Phone: (202) 835-9077 | Email: info@securefreedom.org
For more information, please see securefreedom.org

Book design by Adam Savit
Cover design by Alex VanNess

TABLE OF CONTENTS

FOREWORD

The Muslim Brotherhood has long operated as a formidable political force in Egypt, the place of its founding in 1928, and to varying degrees in other Middle East countries. And as we know, the Muslim Brotherhood has been actively infiltrating American government and society since shortly after the Second World War.

But March 2014 marked a significant step forward for the Brotherhood in America: Some of its key leadership figures joined together to establish the U.S. Council of Muslim Organizations (USCMO), the first political activist group in this country to be openly associated with the jihadist Muslim Brotherhood.

Formation of the USCMO was announced at the National Press Club in Washington, D.C. on 12 March 2014, just blocks from the U.S. Capitol Building. At the podium were: Ousama Jammal, Secretary General USCMO and past President of The Mosque Foundation; Naeem Baig, President, Islamic Circle of North America (ICNA); Nihad Awad, National Executive Director, Council on American-Islamic Relations (CAIR); Mazen Mokhtar, Executive Director, Muslim American Society (MAS); Imam Mahdi Bray, National Director, American Muslim Alliance (AMA); and others associated with identified Muslim Brotherhood organizations.

The significance of this move is best understood in the context of what the Muslim Brotherhood itself calls "civilizational jihad," a term used in its 1991 strategic plan: *An Explanatory Memorandum on the General Strategic Goal of the Group in North America*. As the *Explanatory Memorandum* states, the Brotherhood's mission in America is "destroying Western civilization from within," preparing the way for its replacement by the rule of Islam's supremacist code, shariah (Islamic law). Unlike more immediately violent Brotherhood off-shoots – for example, al-Qa'eda, Egyptian Islamic Jihad, the Islamic State or HAMAS, the Brotherhood in the West has generally taken care to operate stealthily, under the radar, even to the point of sometimes denying its very presence in the United States.

Yet, as the Center for Security Policy's Civilization Jihad Reader Series is documenting, the Muslim Brotherhood's information operations – including many tactics learned from the KGB – have enabled this organization to insinuate itself gradually into a position from which it can assault the pillars of our society. These include: government, academia, faith groups, the media, intelligence and security agencies, our refugee resettlement and other immigration processes and the U.S. judicial system.

By its nature, the object of such a stealthy form of jihad is to ensure that the target community remains unaware of the extent of the threat until it is too late. It is our purpose with this volume and the other monographs of the Center's Civilization Jihad Reader Series to raise the alarm and to engage the American people and their elected representatives in countering this threat while there is still time.

Such an effort has taken on particular urgency in light of the Muslim Brotherhood's launch of an Islamic supremacist "political party" aimed at dramatically ramping up this seditious organization's ability to influence U.S. elections and impact policy. While the numbers of potential voters that such a party could claim to represent are currently relatively small in an electorate the size of America's, it is a worrying prospect that – if effectively marshaled and manipulated – they could have an outsized impact in advancing, both through votes and financial contributions, a Shariah-adherent agenda for the United States.

That is especially problematic since that agenda is rife with hostility to the U.S. Constitution and its established liberties (because Islamists believe that, unlike shariah, they derive from man-made law). Notably, they seek to end the exercise of freedom of speech where it is deemed to be "offensive" to Muslims, a violation of shariah blasphemy restrictions.

The same can be said of the Brotherhood's track record in promoting its shariah agenda sophisticated influence operations against U.S. law enforcement and intelligence agencies, and our government more generally. Were such activities on the part of the USCMO member groups to become even more effective through increased political access and stroke, these Muslim Brotherhood fronts could constitute an even more direct threat to the foundational principles of America, as well as the independence and conduct of our domestic and foreign policy.

In an effort to document the first year of the U.S. Council on Muslim Organization's operations, provide a profile of its key figures and highlight its active role in the development of the next generation of Muslim Brotherhood leadership, the Center for Security Policy initiated a series of reports that were published at the CSP website on a regular basis throughout 2014. That series not only chronicled in real time USCMO organizational, infrastructure-building and political initiatives. It also captured the Council's attempts to obscure those initiatives. Apparently, that was the organization's response upon learning that its operations were being monitored and exposed.

For example, as the Center's series rolled out, USCMO leadership figures such as Sabri Samirah – a veteran member of the Jordanian Muslim Brotherhood who had previously been banned from the United States for a decade (2004-2014) as a national security risk – began to lower their profiles and scrub their exposure on the Internet and social media sites such as Facebook. Such behavior is a further indication, if any were needed, that the USCMO's agenda is *not*, in fact, the sort of benign and patriotic Muslim activism professed by its spokesmen. Instead, it reinforces concerns that this Brotherhood operation is simply opening a new, and particularly ominous, front in the Ikhwan's long-running campaign described in the *Explanatory Memorandum* and aimed at destroying Western civilization and our country "from within."

Star Spangled Shariah: The Rise of America's First Muslim Brotherhood Political Party serves to aggregate and synthesize the insights from that important series of CSP-published articles. We are very proud to present this monograph as the newest addition to the Center's Civilization Jihad Reader Series. Its purpose, beyond enabling the American people and body politic to calibrate this new Muslim Brotherhood enterprise is to showcase how the USCMO can immeasurably help advance the "civilization jihad" and its various, existing influence operations. We intend it to alert citizens, federal, state and local politicians, law enforcement and the broader national security community to the reality that that the supremacist program of the Global Jihad Movement is advancing within U.S. society in a methodical and increasingly insidious manner. It cannot succeed if Americans become aware of what is afoot and vigilant in protecting our civilization, society and Republic against it.

The bottom line is that the Muslim Brotherhood agenda for the United States demonstrably seeks through subversive infiltration of American institutions the triumph of shariah. We are now on notice that U.S. Council of Muslim Organizations is simply the leading edge of the jihadist movement in this country. While the USCMO seeks to cloak itself in red, white, and blue, it is only for the purpose of accomplishing what can aptly be described as "Star Spangled Shariah."

Frank J. Gaffney, Jr.
President and CEO
Center for Security Policy
30 August 2015

INTRODUCTION

By mid-2013, the Muslim Brotherhood experiment in governance was over in Egypt. Despite substantial, official support from the administration of United States President Barack Obama, the Mohamed Morsi regime collapsed within a year of its 2012 election and was replaced by a military regime, headed by Field Marshal Abdel Fatah al-Sisi and supported by much of the Egyptian population. Even as the Brotherhood's 28-year rise to power in Egypt came asunder thanks to Morsi's calamitous rule, key leadership figures among the American Muslim Brotherhood took a major step in announcing the formation of a new political party, the first in U.S. history to be openly associated with the jihadist Muslim Brotherhood. They held a press conference in Washington, DC on 12 March 2014 to announce to formation of the United States Council of Muslim Organizations (USCMO).

This study from the Center for Security Policy, *Star Spangled Shariah: The Rise of America's First Muslim Brotherhood Political Party*, offers an in-depth look at the USCMO's first year of operation. It takes its place among the Center's Civilization Jihad Reader series and offers guidance for private citizens, clergy and community leaders, local, state, and federal law enforcement officers, and elected members at the local, state, and federal levels and their respective staffs about the civilizational jihad mission of the Muslim Brotherhood in America.

FIRST OFFICIAL PRESENCE OF MUSLIM BROTHERHOOD IN THE UNITED STATES

When the Muslim Brotherhood first officially established its presence in the U.S. in 1963 with the formation of the Muslim Student Association (MSA) at the University of Illinois Urbana-Champaign (UIUC) campus, the Brotherhood's settlement process for America began in earnest. The Brotherhood program was counting on the naiveté of too many among U.S. academia, faith-based organizations, legal and law enforcement communities, media, and state and federal elected officials that would allow it to operate openly but unrecognized for the threat it posed to our Constitutional system.

GENERAL STRATEGIC GOAL FOR THE MUSLIM BROTHERHOOD IN NORTH AMERICA

In the landmark 2008 U.S. v Holy Land Foundation, et al. HAMAS terror funding trial, a key Brotherhood document, *An Explanatory Memorandum on the General Strategic Goal for the Group in North America*[1], was entered into evidence as Government Exhibit 003-0085 3:04-CR240-G. This 1991 document, written by Mohamed Akram, a member of the Brotherhood's North American Board of Directors and a senior HAMAS leader, described the Brotherhood's mission in the following way: "The process of settlement is a 'Civilization-Jihadist Process' with all the word means. The Ikhwan [Muslim Brotherhood] must understand that their work in America is a kind of grand jihad in eliminating and destroying Western civilization from within and "sabotaging" its miserable house by their hands and the hands of the believers, so that is eliminated and God's religion is made victorious over all other religions."[2] Clearly, the Muslim Brotherhood agenda for the U.S. includes the subversive infiltration of every sphere of American society and recruitment of assistance in the subversive process from unwitting Americans themselves.

The Muslim Brotherhood understood that successful execution of its plan for societal destruction from within depends on what it calls the "settlement process": "In order for Islam and its Movement" to become "a part of the homeland" in which it lives, "stable" in its land, "rooted" in the spirits and minds of people, "enabled" in the life of its society and firmly-established within organizations through which the Islamic structure is to be built, the Movement must work to obtain "the keys" and tools of this "Civilization Jihadist" project that is the responsibility of the U.S. Muslim Brotherhood.[3]

---

[1] See for full details *From the Archives of the Muslim Brotherhood in America: An Explanatory Memorandum on the General Strategic Goal for the Group in North America* at http://www.centerforsecuritypolicy.org/wp-
[2] "An Explanatory Memorandum on the General Strategic Goals for the Group in North America," as published by the Center for Security Policy. PDF available online at http://www.centerforsecuritypolicy.org/wp-content/uploads/2014/05/Explanatory_Memoradum.pdf
[3] *Ibid*

MUSLIM BROTHERHOOD THEORETICIAN SAYYID QUTB AND MILESTONES

During President Barack Obama's first term (2009-2013), a political climate developed that was more conducive than ever before to advance the Brotherhood's Civilization Jihad and process of settlement that utilize the gradualist framework set forth by the influential Brotherhood theoretician Sayyid Qutb in his seminal 1964 book, 'Milestones.'[4] Despite the fact that these and many other Brotherhood documents are and have been in the hands of U.S. national security agencies for many years, the willingness of senior Obama administration officials to engage in dialogue, outreach, and collaboration with self-identified jihadis continues.

Today, these Muslim Brotherhood organizations which make up the United States Council of Muslim Organizations pose a clear and compelling threat to U.S. national security and the U.S. Constitution. Evidence acquired by American and foreign security agencies documents that the Muslim Brotherhood engages in hostile intelligence collection against U.S. law enforcement and intelligence agencies, and seeks to conduct influence operations (IO) against them and American policymakers.[5] Such activities on the part of these groups constitute a direct threat to the security of the nation's secrets, as well as the independence of its domestic and foreign policy.

This Center for Security Policy study, *Star Spangled Shariah: The Rise of America's First Muslim Brotherhood Political Party*, examines in real time the evolution of the U.S. Council of Muslim Organizations and its development of next generation Muslim Brotherhood leadership in North America. The formation of the USCMO marks the first U.S. Muslim Brotherhood political party, and indeed the first religious identity political party, in the history of this country. Readers will be introduced to the

---

[4] Sayyid Qutb, "Milestones," 2006. Available at http://www.amazon.com/Milestones-Sayed-Qutb/dp/817231244X/ref=tmm_pap_swatch_0?_encoding=UTF8&sr=&qid=
[5] Documents entered into evidence in the 2008 Holy Land Foundation HAMAS terror funding trial are available at the website of the U.S. District Court, Northern District of Texas. http://www.txnd.uscourts.gov/judges/hlf2.html See also Appendix 1 for a description of the "Global Project for Palestine" prepared by the MB in Amman, Jordan. The document instructs the MB to establish intelligence capabilities that include counterintelligence, intelligence collection, and surveillance. Appendix 1 also includes citations from the Charter of the Center of the Studies, the Intelligence and the Information, a document uncovered by Federal Law enforcement at the home of convicted Palestinian Islamic Jihad organizer and Muslim Brotherhood member Sami al-Arian.

leadership of the USCMO from its inception in March 2014 and discover an entity which has operated with a calculated effort to project an image of patriotic transparency, while in fact shrouding its actual anti-Constitutional activities and objectives.

The group's first year's events included the USCMO inaugural banquet in the Washington, D.C. area in June 2014 that featured official representation from two current members of Congress who have been financially supported by the Muslim Brotherhood and whose presentations at that banquet remain unavailable to the public. As the first-ever U.S. Muslim Brotherhood political party began to expand throughout 2014, some of its members participated in anti-Semitic, pro-HAMAS, pro-Muslim Brotherhood demonstrations in the U.S., while also raising funds for Islamic Relief USA, the largest U.S. Muslim charity, and one that sports a troubling history. Beginning to assert itself in the U.S. political arena, the USCMO took aim at Illinois politics during the midterm 2014 election cycle under the vigorous leadership of Sabri Samirah, a veteran member of the Jordanian Muslim Brotherhood who'd previously been banned from the U.S. for a decade (2004-2014) as a national security risk to the U.S.

GRANDSON OF MUSLIM BROTHERHOOD FOUNDER INSPIRES MASSES IN CHICAGO

Nor is Tariq Ramadan, the grandson of Muslim Brotherhood founder Hassan al-Banna, any stranger to the USCMO. In January 2010, Secretary of State Hillary Clinton gifted the U.S. Muslim Brotherhood a key opportunity when she signed an order that lifted the ban that had prohibited Ramadan from entering the U.S. for the previous six years.[6] Ramadan now could finally enter the United States for the first time since the Department of Homeland Security revoked his visa in July 2004 during the administration of President George W. Bush.

On 21 December 2012, Tariq Ramadan issued a prescient directive to the Muslim Brotherhood leadership while participating at the 11th Annual Muslim American Society-Islamic Circle of North America (MAS-ICNA) Convention in Chicago, Illinois:

> So this is why Muslims when they say we are at home should institutionalize the presence in the country…We are at home, show it! Not show it with what you say, show it with the institutions you

---

[6] "U.S. Government Lifts Ban on Tariq Ramadan," a blog entry posted by Tariq Ramadan to his website at http://tariqramadan.com/blog/2010/01/20/us-government-lifts-ban-on-tariq-ramadan/, accessed 17 March 2014

have in this country – institutionalize the Muslim presence as Americans. This is home; this is where we can say 'that's where we are'...I think we are reconciling the West with the very essence of our universal principles – if we understand Islam the right way, if we understand why we are experiencing this historical moment of the Muslim presence in the West.7

We are witnesses in real time to a new development in the 'Civilization-Jihadist Process' set in motion by the Muslim Brotherhood through the U.S. Council of Muslim Organizations. The establishment of this group in fact operationalizes the Brotherhood responsibility to pursue 'Civilization Jihad' in the U.S. in a specifically political way. With this Reader, the Center hopes to inform citizens, law enforcement, legislators, and national security officers alike about that process, help them to understand its subversive implications, and encourage America's appointed and elected representatives to focus close attention on this latest initiative from the U.S. Muslim Brotherhood.

GENESIS OF THE U.S. COUNCIL OF MUSLIM ORGANIZATIONS

Executive leadership from some of the most prominent American Muslim organizations announced the formation of the United States Council of Muslim Organizations (USCMO) on Wednesday, 12 March 2014 at the National Press Club in Washington, DC.[8] The eight founding Muslim organizations participating at the press conference9 were immediately joined by two additional U.S. Muslim organizations. Key Muslim leadership representatives spoke about the vision and mission of the USCMO and appeared in the following order:

* **Ousama Jammal**, Secretary General USCMO and past President of The Mosque Foundation
* **Naeem Baig**, President, Islamic Circle of North America (ICNA)
* **Nihad Awad**, National Executive Director, Council on American-Islamic Relations (CAIR)
* **Mazen Mokhtar**, Executive Director, Muslim American Society (MAS)
* **Imam W. Deen Mohammed II**, President, The Mosque Cares (grandson of the NOI founder)

---

[7] Notes from Muslim American Society-Islamic Circle of North America Annual Chicago Convention, December 2012

[8] U.S. Council of Muslim Organizations, "Announcing the Formation of the US Council of Muslim Organizations," http://uscmo.org/, accessed 14 March 2014

[9] CAIRtv, "Major Muslim Groups Launch New Council at D.C. News Conference," http://www.youtube.com/watch?v=BsQeflNzO94/, accessed 14 March 2014

* **Khalil Meek**, Executive Director, Muslim Legal Fund of America (MLFA)
* **Imam Mahdi Bray**, National Director, American Muslim Alliance (AMA)
* **Osama Abu-irshaid**, National Board Member, American Muslims for Palestine (AMP)
* **Imam Talib Abdur-Rashid**, Deputy Emir, Muslim Alliance in North America (MANA)
* **Mahdabuddin Ahmad**, Director of Community Affairs, Muslim Ummah of North America (MUNA)

The USCMO is described as an umbrella organization – and CAIR Executive Director Nihad Awad inferred that and more, with his assertion regarding the USCMO that "This is the dream of every American Muslim, to unify the approach, agenda and vision of the Muslim community. In the past, many people have tried to unite on a limited agenda, but this is a broad agenda for the American Muslim community." Awad stressed the need for a "platform to coordinate, to communicate, and unify the vision on critical issues both to the Muslim community and the society at large," because he believes that "Muslim voters can be swing voters in key elections, especially 2016." The formation of the USCMO marks the first U.S. Muslim Brotherhood political party, and indeed the first religious identity political party in the history of this country.

MUSLIM BROTHERHOOD FRONT GROUPS

USCMO founding members CAIR and ICNA were previously identified as front groups for the Muslim Brotherhood during the Holy Land Foundation (HLF)[10] trial in 2007. Sheikh Kifah Mustapha, who has worked with Ousama Jammal (current Mosque Foundation board member) at The Mosque Foundation, was listed by name as an unindicted co-conspirator in the HLF trial as a member of the Muslim Brotherhood's Palestine Committee. According to documents entered into evidence at the HLF trial, he was a "registered agent for HLF in Illinois" who acknowledged fundraising for the HLF from the mid-1990s until 2001. Mustapha has also raised money for MAS and ICNA initiatives during their annual conferences in Chicago.

---

[10] United States District Court, Northern District of Texas, *USA v. Holy Land Foundation for Relief and Development* Exhibit List, http://www.txnd.uscourts.gov/judges/hlf2.html

It is important to note the geo-political influence of the Muslim Brotherhood in Illinois, as this relates to the oversight of USCMO's eight founding member organizations.

USCMO MEMBER ORGANIZATIONS WITH HEADQUARTERS IN ILLINOIS

* The Mosque Foundation[11] (7360 W. 93rd Street, Bridgeview IL 60455)
* American Muslims for Palestine[12] (10101 South Roberts Road, Palos Hills, IL 60465)
* The Mosque Cares[13] (929 West 171st Street, Hazel Crest, IL 60429)

USCMO MEMBER ORGANIZATIONS WITH REGIONAL OFFICES IN ILLINOIS

* Islamic Circle of North America[14] (6224 N. California Avenue, Chicago, IL 60659)
* Council on American Islamic Relations Chicago[15] (17 N. State Street, Suite 1500, Chicago, Illinois 60602)
* Muslim American Society[16] (9210 South Oketo Avenue, Bridgeview, IL 60455)
* Muslim Legal Fund of America[17] (15255 S. 94th Ave, 5th Floor, Orland Park, IL 60462)

During the press conference, Nihad Awad indicated his organization CAIR was "proud to join this historic organization, because today is a historic one. We have been meeting for at least one and a half years." However, the information absent from this discussion by Awad and his colleagues was that the development of the USCMO not only predates the eighteen month time frame, but finds its origins in the Chicago

---

[11] The Mosque Foundation http://www.mosquefoundation.org/, accessed 14 March 2014
[12] American Muslims for Palestine, http://www.ampalestine.org/, accessed 14 March 2014
[13] The Mosque Cares, A Ministry of W. Deen Mohammed, http://www.ministryofwdeenmohammed.org/, accessed 12 March 2014
[14] Islamic Circle of North America Chicago, http://www.icnachicago.org/, accessed 14 March 2014
[15] Council on American Islamic Relations Chicago, http://www.cairchicago.org/, accessed 14 March 2014
[16] Muslim American Society, https://www.muslimamericansociety.org/, accessed 14 March 2014
[17] Muslim Legal Fund of America https://www.mlfa.org/, accessed 14 March 2014

metropolitan area, where the Muslim Brotherhood has successfully built a strategic organizational network for almost six decades.[18]

On 20 January 2010[19], Secretary of State Hillary Rodham Clinton gifted the U.S. Muslim Brotherhood a key opportunity when she signed the Exercise of Discretionary Authority under Section 212(d)(3)(B)(i) of the Immigration and Nationality Act.[20] Tariq Ramadan, the grandson of Muslim Brotherhood founder Hassan al Banna, now could finally enter the United States for the first time since the Department of Homeland Security revoked his visa in July 2004 during the administration of President George W. Bush.

PROJECT MOBILIZE

Less than four months later, on 5 May 2010, Project Mobilize[21] (also known as Project M), which included board members with ties to multiple Muslim Brotherhood front organizations, was founded by M. Yasser Tabara[22] in Summit, Illinois. USCMO Secretary General Ousama Jammal was a founding Board Member of Project Mobilize. M. Yasser Tabara, Project Mobilize President, was former executive director for CAIR Chicago. Project Mobilize board member Safaa Zarzour, Esq.[23] is former Secretary General of the Islamic Society of North America. Two Project Mobilize board members, Dr. Mohammed Zaher Sahloul and Safaa

---

[18] Mosque Foundation, "History and Timeline," http://www.mosquefoundation.org/about-us/history-timeline, accessed 14 March 2014

[19] Steven Emerson, The Investigative Project on Terrorism, "Apologists or Extremists: Tariq Ramadan," 8 March 2010. http://www.investigativeproject.org/profile/111#_ftnref12

[20] U.S. Department of Homeland Security, U.S. Citizenship and Immigration Services, "Exercise of Discretionary Authority under Section 212(d)(3)(B)(i) of the Immigration and Nationality Act," 23 January 2010. http://www.uscis.gov/sites/default/files/USCIS/Outreach/Notes%20from%20Previo us%20Engagements/MEMO%20-%20Implementation%20of%20New%20Discretionary%20Exemption.pdf

[21] Project Mobilize Non-Profit Organization Facebook Page, https://www.facebook.com/pages/Project-Mobilize/108921129167785?id=108921129167785&sk=info, accessed 20 June 2013

[22] Council on American Islamic Relations Chicago, "Our Board," http://www.cairchicago.org/our-board/yaser-tabbara/, accessed 21 March 2014

[23] Zakat Foundation of America, "ZF Welcomes Former Secretary General of ISNA to Staff," 7 February 2013. http://www.zakat.org/news/zf-welcomes-former-secretary-general-of-isna-to-staff/, accessed 25 February 2013

Zarzour, Esq. were appointed[24] to the American Muslim Advisory Council[25] on 30 August 2011 by Illinois Governor Patrick Quinn.

In April 2010, Tariq Ramadan returned to the US where he was keynote speaker and the 6th Annual CAIR-Chicago Banquet[26] [27] and addressed members of the Council on Islamic Organizations of Greater Chicago (CIOGC). In July 2010 and July 1011, Ramadan was a keynote speaker for both the 47th annual ISNA[28] and the 48th annual ISNA[29] conventions in Chicago. In December 2012 and December 2013, Ramadan was a keynote speaker for the 11th annual MAS-ICNA[30] and 12th annual MAS-ICNA[31] conventions in Chicago, where he has communicated the need for Muslim American integration and participation in the political process and society.

At the Project Mobilize website[32] [33], its stated mission included the following:

[24] Illinois Government News Network: Governor's Office Press Release, "Governor Quinn Announces Creation of Muslim American Advisory Council Names Members to New Council During Religious Observance," 30 August 2011. http://www3.illinois.gov/PressReleases/ShowPressRelease.cfm?SubjectID=3&RecNum=9697

[25] State of Illinois, American Muslim American Advisory Council, "Membership," http://www2.illinois.gov/gov/MAAC/Pages/membership.aspx

[26] Council on American Islamic Relations Chicago, "Thank You for a Record-Breaking Banquet!" 14 April 2010. http://www.cairchicago.org/2010/04/14/thank-you-for-a-record-breaking-banquet-see-photos/, accessed 23 March 2014

[27] Noreen S. Ahmed-Ullah, "On U.S. speaking tour, once-banned Muslim scholar Tariq Ramadan shares his vision for the future," *Chicago Tribune*, 23 April 2010. http://articles.chicagotribune.com/2010-04-23/opinion/ct-oped-0423-ramadan-20100423_1_muslim-brotherhood-muslim-scholar-american-muslims

[28] Muslim Public Affairs Council, "Join MPAC at ISNA's 47th Annual Convention This Weekend," 1 July 2010. http://www.mpac.org/events/join-mpac-at-47th-annual-isna-convention-this-weekend.php#.U1Xyf1cs0TB, accessed 29 March 2014

[29] Maqbool Ahmed Siraj, "48th Annual [sic] ISNA Convention at Chicago: Meeting the Challenge of Pluralism," *Islamic Voice*, August 2011. http://tariqramadan.com/english/ai1ec_event/mas-icna-12-th-annual-convention/?instance_id=, accessed 29 March 2014

[30] MAS-ICNA Convention YouTube Channel, "2012 MAS-ICNA Convention Guest Speakers," 8 November 2012. https://www.youtube.com/watch?v=urC3JgVlUos, accessed 29 March 2014

[31] Tariq Ramadan, "MAS-ICNA 12th annual convention," December 2012. http://tariqramadan.com/english/ai1ec_event/mas-icna-12-th-annual-convention/?instance_id=

[32] Project Mobilize, http://www.projectmobilize.org, accessed 22 May 2011

* To Develop the political capital existing within the Muslim American community;
* To Organize the Muslim American community around issues determined relevant; and
* To Advocate on behalf of the Muslim American community to elected officials and persons with political clout so that they act upon the concerns and desires of their Muslim American constituents.

In the Company Overview from their Facebook page[34], Project Mobilize described itself as "Based in the Chicagoland area, Project Mobilize or Project M is a non-profit political action and civic engagement organization dedicated to the education, development, and political advancement of the Muslim American community locally, statewide, and across the country."

In April 2011, Project Mobilize successfully fielded its first candidates[35] for political office: Asif Yusuf was elected as Oakbrook Village trustee; Ahmed Aduib was elected to the Bridgeview library board; Nuha Hasan was elected as a Village of Justice park district commissioner. Four years earlier in 2007, the Chicago Council on Global Affairs sponsored a study about political and civic participation, which included the Muslim American community. Project Mobilize stated that "among the top three recommendations of this diverse task force was to increase the civic participation of the Muslim American population beyond its current scope. This principle mirrors the fundamental objective of Project M and its three-pronged mission."

In the Project Mobilize website[36] section "Why Us? Why Now?" it is clear that Project Mobilize was the genesis for the formation of the USCMO: *"There is political talent in the Muslim American community that needs only direction and resources in order to gain substantive footing."* Project Mobilize leadership intended for itself to be a catalyst for political action: *"The long and extensive history of mobilization by several local Muslim-*

---

[33] Council on American Islamic Relations Chicago, "CAIR-Chicago Says Goodbye to Reema Ahmad," http://www.cairchicago.org/2011/01/18/cair-chicago-says-goodbye-to-reema-ahmad/, accessed 21 January 2011

[34] Project Mobilize Facebook Page, https://www.facebook.com/pages/Project-Mobilize/108921129167785?id=108921129167785&sk=info, accessed 30 June 2011

[35] Meha Ahmad, "Muslims get elected to public office," *Chicago Crescent,* http://www.chicagocrescent.com/crescent/columnistArticlesMeha2.php?nTitle=Muslims%20get%20elected%20to%20public%20office, accessed 4 May 2011

[36] Project Mobilize Website, "Why Us, Why Now?" http://www.projectmobilize.org/about/why-us-why-now/, accessed 30 June 2011

membered organizations has adequately laid the foundation for more strategic and consistent organizing efforts in the future."

In President Barack Obama's first term, the Muslim Brotherhood in the United States began to experience a political climate more conducive to their advancement of Civilization Jihad[37] in accordance with the framework articulated by influential Muslim Brotherhood theologian Sayyid Qutb in his book Milestones.[38] Project Mobilize affirmed this reality on their website: "And finally, the political climate is ripe for an organization that will pave the way for concentrated advocacy efforts in the name of the Muslim American community." The Project Mobilize leadership tactically positioned itself looking long term with the eventual formation of the USCMO coming to fruition in March 2014.

As the 2016 presidential election cycle heats up, the USCMO initiative to fortify Muslim citizenship rights "by conducting a census of American Muslims to create a database that will be used to enhance civic and political participation in upcoming elections," shows all the outward signs that the Muslim Brotherhood actively is working to create the equivalent of the Republican Party's GOP Data Center, formerly known as Voter Vault.

In order to better understand the formative dynamics of USCMO leadership, the following chapter examines the role and influence of USCMO Secretary General Oussama Jammal prior to the official formation of the first political party in U.S. history to be openly associated with the jihadist Muslim Brotherhood. In 2009, U.S. President Barack Obama began to implement his agenda of "fundamentally transforming the United States of America" in ways that advanced the Brotherhood's 'civilization jihad' agenda at home and empowered its revolutions abroad.

Despite warnings from key members of Congress, who tried in 2012 to call attention to the subversion with letters to the Inspectors General of the Office of the Director of National Intelligence and Departments of Defense, Homeland Security, Justice, and State, the Obama administration doggedly pressed ahead with its Brotherhood-friendly policies. From drawing into his administration advisors and appointees with Brotherhood connections to turning U.S. foreign policy on its head to favor the rise of Muslim Brotherhood regimes to power, President Obama's policies were a welcome change for Jammal, the USCMO, and the American Muslim Brotherhood.

---

[37] Center for Security Policy, "The Muslim Brotherhood in America: A Course in 10 Parts Presented by Frank Gaffney," http://www.centerforsecuritypolicy.org/the-muslim-brotherhood-in-america/

[38] Studies in Islam and the Middle East Electronic Books, "Milestones by Sayyid AQutb," http://majalla.org/books/2005/qutb-nilestone.pdf, accessed 9 April 2014

U.S. DEPARTMENT OF STATE RECRUITMENT AT MUSLIM BROTHERHOOD CONVENTION

The United States Muslim Brotherhood political party, the United States Council of the Muslim Organizations (USCMO), was established in March 2014, but its top leadership, including USCMO Secretary General Oussama Jammal, had launched into political activism long before then. As this chapter will demonstrate, that political activism by Muslim Brotherhood-linked operatives has the open support of the U.S. Department of State.

One earlier event that now stands out more in retrospect than it might have at the time was the 11th annual Muslim American Society-Islamic Circle of North America Muslim Brotherhood convention that was held in Chicago in December 2012. The convention's theme, "Toward a Renaissance: Believe, Act, & Engage," foreshadowed the political activism to come. Today the USCMO Secretary General, Jammal at the time of the 2012 MAS-ICNA convention already was a national-level leader of the Brotherhood-linked MAS as well as the Bridgeview, Illinois-based Mosque Foundation and played an active role as speaker and discussion moderator at the event.

USCMO SECRETARY GENERAL OUSSAMA JAMMAL AND MUSLIM BROTHERHOOD NEXUSES

In addition to his current leadership role overseeing the operations of the USCMO, Oussama Jammal is the vice president of the Mosque Foundation, where he was once the president. Two among the Mosque Foundation's current leaders, Sheikh Jamal Said and Sheik Kifah Mustapha, were named as unindicted, coconspirators in the Holy Land Foundation (HLF) Hamas financing trial in Texas, which concluded in late 2008 with a unanimous guilty verdict on 108 counts. Additionally, Jammal serves on the MAS National Executive Council; he is also the Executive Director for Illinois MAS Public Affairs and Civic Engagement (PACE). The MAS presents itself as "a non-profit 501(C)(3) organization," and "a dynamic charitable, religious, social, cultural, and educational, organization" with a mission "to move people to strive for God consciousness, liberty, and justice, and to convey Islam with utmost clarity."

In fact, however, the MAS was established in 1993 by the Muslim Brotherhood "whose goal is the "introduction of the Islamic Shari`ah as the basis controlling the affairs of state and society." The MAS also happens to be a founding member of the USCMO. Positive references to so-called 'martyrdom operations' have featured in the MAS magazine The American Muslim, which contains fatwas issued by various Islamic scholars including Yusuf al-Qaradawi (senior jurist of the Muslim Brotherhood) and Muhammad al-Hanooti. A 2001 FBI memorandum stated that al-Hanooti, who attended the 1993 Philadelphia meeting of U.S.-based HAMAS members and supporters that led to the establishment of CAIR (Council on American Islamic Relations), raised over $6 million for HAMAS.

So, this was the political milieu for the December 2012 MAS-ICNA conference. The photocopy[39] of the following speakers list reads like a Who's Who of notables from the U.S. Muslim activist scene with long-established links to the Muslim Brotherhood.

2012 SPEAKERS

Abdelgawad Konsouh	Jamaal Diwan	Omer Muzaffar
Abdul Fattah Mourou	Karen Danielson	Osama Abu-Irshaid
Abdur Rahman Khan	Khalil Meek	Osman Osman
Ahmed Mirza	Khalilah Sabra	Oussama Jammal
Altaf Husain	Kifah Mustapha	Ragheb Elsergany
Amal Ali	Mark Ward	Sabeel Ahmed
Amjad Qourshah	Mohamed Husain Isa	Safaa Zarzour
Ayed Al-Qarni	Mohamed Alnutaleb	Siraj Wahhaj
Ayman Hammous	Mohammad Qatanani	Suhaib Webb
Bassam Estwani	Mokhtar Maghraoui	Talib Shareef
Edmund Arroyo	Montaser Maral	Tariq Ramadan
Habeeb Quadri	Muslema Purmul	W.D. Muhammad Jr
Hamed Ghazali	Mustafa Housny	Yusuf Estes
Hatem Bazian	Nabil Chbib	Zahid Bukhari
Imad Bayoun	Naeem Baig	Zaid Shakir
Mohamed Magid	Nihad Awad	
Jamal Badawi	Omar Atia	

Speakers list for 11th Annual MAS-ICNA Convention, Chicago, IL December 2012

One whose presence among such a gathering fairly begs for explanation is Mark S. Ward, the Deputy Special Coordinator in the Office of Middle East Transition, Office of the Deputy Secretary. Not only was Ward a featured speaker at this Muslim Brotherhood event, as can be seen

---

[39] 11th Annual Muslim American Society-Islamic Circle of North America Convention Program Book

24

from the official speakers list above, but he used the podium that day to solicit recruits from among the Muslim Brotherhood-dominated audience for employment with the State Department Foreign Service and U.S. Agency for International Development (USAID).

Following are photocopies[40] of sections from page 10 of the MAS-ICNA convention program booklet that show Mark Ward's presentation slot (which he shared with Ayman Hammous and Oussama Jammal) and a short description of his topic about encouraging Muslim youth to pursue careers with the State Department.

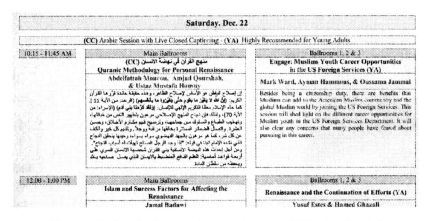

"Engage: Muslims Youth Career Opportunities in the US Foreign Service"

At this session, Ward and Ayman Hammous (current MAS Board of Trustee member) were introduced by Oussama Jammal. Ayman Hammous spoke first, emphasizing that Islam is a message to humanity and stressing the importance of building bridges between the East and West. He spoke about how it is the mission of American Muslims to fulfill the message of Qur'an, so that a Muslim one day could become Secretary of State or even U.S. President. When Ward began his presentation, he told the audience that even though they may be at odds with U.S. foreign policy in the Islamic world, the way to change that is by joining the government to help change things from the inside.

He told the audience the best way to address problems Muslims may have with US foreign policy was to have Muslims work from the inside to change it, telling them that he wanted them in the Foreign Service for the languages, culture, and skill sets they possessed and assuring his Muslim Brotherhood audience that they would not be treated any differently in terms

---

[40] Ibid

of the required security clearances than any other applicants. He added that as it is now, the U.S. government looked too much like him and not enough like them. He next spoke about his career and deep friendship with slain U.S. Ambassador to Libya, J. Christopher Stevens, with whom he worked directly for several months. Ward concluded with an overview of the work of the Department of State and USAID and explained the role of Foreign Service officers. Throughout the course of the presentation by Ward, Oussama Jammal fielded questions from the audience in addition to posing a number of his own questions.

Judicial Watch (JW), the non-profit watchdog group, has been seeking State Department records related to that speech by Mark Ward since first filing an initial Freedom of Information Act (FOIA) request in January 2013. On 4 April 2013, JW filed a follow-up lawsuit, *Judicial Watch v. U.S. Department of State*[41]_(No. 1:13-cv-00593), to obtain the documents. A month later, JW noted[42] that although required by law to respond by 7 March 2013, as of 2 May 2013 "the department has failed to produce any records responsive to the request, indicate when any responsive records will be produced, or demonstrated that responsive records are exempt from production." Given that Ward was surrounded at this event by other speakers known for links to the jihadist Muslim Brotherhood, itself the parent organization of both al-Qa'eda and HAMAS, the State Department's reluctance to admit to a targeted recruitment operation among such a potential employee pool is understandable. Its refusal to comply with legal requirements to do so will be adjudicated by a judge.

---

[41] *Judicial Watch v. U.S. Department of State*, Case 1:13-cv-00593, 26 April 2013. http://www.scribd.com/doc/138909146/Stamped-Complaint/

[42] Judicial Watch, "JW Sues Obama State Department for Talking Points and Updates Given to Susan Rice Related to Benghazi Attack,"23 July 2013. http://www.judicialwatch.org/press-room/press-releases/judicial-watch-sues-obama-state-department-for-talking-points-and-updates-given-to-susan-rice-related-to-benghazi-attack/

The photocopy[43] of the next program section below shows Ward's second presentation topic, "U.S.-Muslim Relations in the Wake of the Arab Spring," for which he shared the time slot with Hatem Bazian[44], a former student leader of the Brotherhood's Muslim Students Association (MSA) at his U.C. Berkeley campus and an outspoken anti-Semitic, anti-Israel supporter of Palestinian statehood.

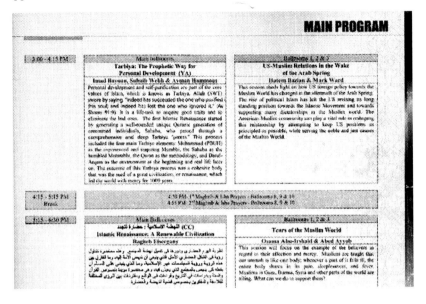

"US Muslim Relations in the Wake of the Arab Spring"

The MAS-ICNA convention held at the Sheraton Chicago Hotel and Towers from 21-25 December 2012 wasn't the first such event to which the State Department sent Mark Ward, however. In fact, two weeks following the deadly attacks on the American mission in Benghazi, Libya, the MAS PACE held its First American Muslim Leadership Conference from 24-26 September 2012 at a Marriott hotel in Teaneck, New Jersey—and Mark S. Ward was a guest speaker. His biography was included on the MAS website[45] alongside nationally and internationally recognized members of the Muslim Brotherhood leadership. The theme, "Charting the Way Ahead," addressed U.S. and Muslim World Relations.

---

[43] Ibid
[44] CAMERA on Campus, "Hatem Bazian,"
http://www.cameraoncampus.org/campus-figures/hatem-bazian/#.VTq463ktGM9
[45] Muslim American Society Public Affairs and Civics Engagement, "Speaker's Biography," http://www.maspace.org/speakers-bios.html, accessed 21 November 2014

The MAS Chicago Chapter[46] posted the photo below of Mark S. Ward at the MAS PACE leadership conference in New Jersey. Pictured from left to right are Hussein Ata (President, Mosque Foundation in Bridgeview), Karen Danielson (MAS PACE), Mark S. Ward, and Oussama Jammal (Chairman MAS PACE). As the December 2012 MAS-ICNA convention would do in Chicago just three months later, this event likewise featured key Muslim Brotherhood operatives preparing their top leadership figures for the political activism that the USCMO shortly would take up as the first Brotherhood political party in U.S. history. And the State Department's Office of Middle East Transition, then in the midst of championing the rise to power of Egypt's first Muslim Brotherhood president (Mohamed Morsi), didn't want to miss a chance to encourage a similar agenda for the U.S. political scene.

MAS PACE First American Muslim Leadership Conference
"CHARTING THE WAY AHEAD"

The Zakat Foundation of America (ZFA) was the sponsor for this first MAS PACE leadership conference. ZFA, founded in 2001, is

[46] Muslim American Society – MAS – Chicago Chapter Facebook Page Timeline Photos, "MAS PACE First American Muslim Leadership Conference CHARTING THE WAY AHEAD September 24 - 26, 2012" https://mbasic.facebook.com/maschicago/photos/a.120550404631131.16506.11498 7765187395/489709031048598/?type=1&source=46&refid=17, accessed 21 November 2014

headquartered in Worth, Illinois. Its billboard[47] below is prominently displayed in a highly-trafficked area in the western suburbs of Chicago, as shown in the following photo:

Zakat Foundation billboard in western suburbs of Chicago

U.S. PRESIDENT BARACK OBAMA'S COMMITMENT TO SUPPORT ZAKAT

It seems relevant to note that during his "A New Beginning[48]" speech in Cairo in June 2009, U.S. President Barack Obama stated, "In the United States, rules on charitable giving have made it harder for Muslims to fulfill their religious obligation. That is why I am committed to working with American Muslims to ensure that they can fulfill *zakat*." Unfortunately, the President conveniently glossed right over the key fact that '*zakat*' is not merely 'charity,' but rather an obligatory annual tax on all Muslim individuals and firms, a fixed percentage of whose proceeds Islamic Law requires be donated to jihad.

Andrew McCarthy, former Chief Assistant U.S. Attorney in New York, best known for leading the Justice Department prosecution against the

---

[47] Photo is property of Center for Security Policy, July 2014
[48] THE WHITE HOUSE Office of the Press Secretary (Cairo, Egypt), "REMARKS BY THE PRESIDENT ON A NEW BEGINNING, Cairo University, Cairo, Egypt," 4 June 2009. https://www.whitehouse.gov/blog/NewBeginning/transcripts

Blind Sheik, Omar Abdel Rahman, points out that only Muslims can be the recipients of *zakat*. He also notes[49] the Qur'anic-based explanation that "Muslims are taught that charity means Muslims aiding Muslims, for the purpose of fortifying and extending the *ummah* [Muslim community] until all the world is Islam's domain."

MUSLIM BROTHERHOOD INFLUENCE OPERATIONS AND CIVILIZATION JIHAD

Nearly seven months before the December 2012 MAS-ICNA convention, on 13 June 2012, Congresswoman Michele Bachmann (R-MN), Congressman Trent Franks (R-AZ)[50], Congressman Louie Gohmert (R-TX), Congressman Tom Rooney (R-FL), and Congressman Westmoreland (R-GA) sent letters to the Inspectors General of the Office of the Director of National Intelligence (ODNI), the Department of Defense (DoD), the Department of Homeland Security (DHS), the Department of Justice (DoJ), and the Department of State (DoS) seeking to obtain answers to pressing national security questions about the extent of the Muslim Brotherhood's activities within the U.S. government. Copies of the letters are available here: Office of the Director of National Intelligence[51], the Department of Defense[52], the Department of Homeland Security[53], the Department of Justice[54] and the Department of State[55].

In their communication with Ambassador Harold W. Geisel at the U.S Department of State, these five members of Congress, known as the "National Security Five," presented their concerns about potential threats to U.S. security as a result of influence operations being run by the Muslim

---

[49] Andrew C. McCarthy, "Uncharitable," *National Review*, 23 April 2011. http://www.nationalreview.com/article/265437/uncharitable-andrew-c-mccarthy
[50] Please reference for additional background Congressman Trent Franks Statement on IG Letters Concerning Muslim Brotherhood, 24 July 2012. https://franks.house.gov/press-release/franks-statement-ig-letters-concerning-muslim-brotherhood
[51] http://bachmann.house.gov/sites/bachmann.house.gov/files/UploadedFiles/IG_Letter_ODNI.pdf
[52] http://bachmann.house.gov/sites/bachmann.house.gov/files/UploadedFiles/IG_Letter_DOD.pdf
[53] http://bachmann.house.gov/sites/bachmann.house.gov/files/UploadedFiles/IG_Letter_DHS.pdf
[54] http://bachmann.house.gov/sites/bachmann.house.gov/files/UploadedFiles/IG_Letter_DOJ.pdf
[55] http://bachmann.house.gov/sites/bachmann.house.gov/files/UploadedFiles/IG_Letter_Dept_of_State.pdf

Brotherhood and its affiliates in the United States. This is how the letter[56] began:

Congress of the United States
Washington, DC 20515

June 13, 2012

Ambassador Harold W. Geisel
Deputy Inspector General
Department of State
2201 C Street, N.W.
Washington, DC 20520

Dear Ambassador Geisel:

As you may know, information has recently come to light that raises serious questions about Department of State policies and activities that appear to be a result of influence operations conducted by individuals and organizations associated with the Muslim Brotherhood. Given that the U.S. government has established in federal court[1] that the Muslim Brotherhood's mission in the United States is "destroying the Western civilization from within" – a practice the Muslim Brothers call "civilization jihad" – we believe that the apparent involvement of those with such ties raises serious security concerns that warrant your urgent attention.

Opening statement referencing Muslim Brotherhood and its "Civilization Jihad"

The "National Security Five" included in their letter citations from Brotherhood documents that had been presented as evidence by the DoJ prosecutors in federal court[57] [58] in the 2008 Holy Land Foundation HAMAS terror funding trial that established the mission of the Muslim Brotherhood in the West as one of Civilization Jihad[59]:

> "The process of settlement is a 'Civilization-Jihadist Process' with all the word means. The Ikhwan must understand that their work in America is a kind of grand jihad in eliminating and destroying

---

[56] Screenshot of Letter from congressional website of U.S. Representative Michele Bachmann, accessed 21 November 2014

[57] Center for Security Policy, "An Explanatory Memorandum: From the Archives of the Muslim Brotherhood in America,"25 March 2013.
http://www.centerforsecuritypolicy.org/2013/05/25/an-explanatory-memorandum-from-the-archives-of-the-muslim-brotherhood-in-america/

[58] Please reference the government's evidence in the Holy Land Foundation Trial, N.D. TX (2008), specifically "An Explanatory Memorandum for on the Strategic Goal for the Group in North America ," and see *United States v. Holy Land Foundation et al.* (No. 09-10875)(2010). For a partial list of exhibits, please see http://www.txnd.uscourts.gov/judges/hlf2.html

[59] The Investigative Project on Terrorism, "Government Exhibit 003-0085 3:04-CR-240-G *U.S. v. HLF, et al*," http://www.investigativeproject.org/documents/misc/20.pdf

the Western civilization from within and 'sabotaging' its miserable house by their hands and the hands of the believers so that it is eliminated and God's religion is made victorious over all other religions."

When the U.S. State Department reaches out pro-actively to recruit Muslim Brotherhood supporters for the Foreign Service and a career path, complete with Top Secret security clearance, that could lead eventually to top positions in U.S. policymaking circles, but refuses to admit publicly what it is doing, alarm bells should sound. After the Inspectors General of both the State Department and Intelligence Community were warned explicitly by Congressional members concerned for the nation's vulnerability about Muslim Brotherhood infiltration and influence operations, there can be no excuse that they just didn't know.

As of April 2015, the Department of State website still lists Mark S. Ward[60] as the Deputy Special Coordinator in the Office of Middle East Transition, Office of the Deputy Secretary.

USCMO Secretary General Oussama Jammal has a well-established track record of political activism and success at developing strategic relationships for the benefit of the Muslim Brotherhood with members of the U.S. government. After the official formation of the USCMO, Jammal wasted no time in preparing an historic gathering of Brotherhood leadership and government officials for their inaugural banquet in the Washington, D.C. area.

---

[60] U.S. Department of State, "Mark S. Ward, Deputy Special Coordinator in the Office of Middle East Transition, Office of the Deputy Secretary," http://www.state.gov/r/pa/ei/biog/bureau/194564.htm, accessed 1 April 2015

U.S. MUSLIM BROTHERHOOD POLITICAL PARTY CONVENES FOR INAUGURAL BANQUET

Weeks following the March 2014 announcement in Washington, D.C. by executive leadership from some of the most prominent American Muslim organizations about their formation of the United States Council of Muslim Organizations (USCMO), the U.S. Muslim Brotherhood political party, and indeed the first religious identity political party in the history of this country, began preparing for its inaugural banquet[61] to be held at the Hilton Crystal City Hotel on Tuesday, 10 June 2014.

Invite for event which no longer appears on USCMO website[62]

While limited information exists regarding the actual content of speeches and proceedings from the USCMO inaugural banquet, the Muslim Link Paper[63] reported nearly "250 guests of the member organizations, leaders and imams of masajid, elected and government officials, dignitaries, civic and interfaith partners attended the banquet." Two members of the

---

[61] United States Council of Muslim Organizations, "USCMO Inauguration - June 10, 2014," http://www.uscmo.org/inauguration/, accessed 19 June 2014

[62] Ibid

[63] The Muslim Link, "New Umbrella Group Holds Inaugural Banquet," http://www.muslimlinkpaper.com/community-news/community-news/3679-new-umbrella-group-holds-inaugural-banquet.html, accessed 19 June 2014

U.S. Congress, Representatives André Carson (Democrat, IN-7ᵗʰ District), Keith Ellison (Democrat, MN-5ᵗʰ District), and Hassan El-Amin, Associate Judge, Prince George's County Circuit Court, 7ᵗʰ Judicial Circuit (Maryland) joined together on the speaker's dais with Muslim Brotherhood leadership to address the attendees.

Inaugural USCMO banquet guest "selfie" photo with Congressman Andre Carson[64]

The founding leaders of USCMO react to Congressman Keith Ellison's address[65]

---

[64] Ibid
[65] Ibid

ICNA Relief's board chairman Mohsin Ansari talks to Congressman Keith Ellison[66]

US Congressmen Keith Ellison and Andre Carson with USCMO leadership[67]

---

[66] ICNA Relief USA, "ICNA Relief USA Only Muslim Charity Invited to Speak at Formation of U.S. Council of Muslim Organizations," http://www.icnarelief.org/site2/index.php/blog-post/disaster-relief-efforts/502-icna-relief-usa-only-muslim-charity-invited-to-speak-at-formation-of-u-s-council-of-muslim-organizations, accessed 23 June 2014
[67] Ibid

As reported by the USCMO, confirmed speakers[68] for its inaugural banquet included the following:

Congressman Andre Carson

Congressman Keith Ellison

Prof. Suleiman Nyang

Dr. Ihsan Bagby

---

[68] United States Council of Muslim Organizations, USCMO Inauguration - June 10, 2014: Confirmed Speakers at the Inaugural Event,"
http://www.uscmo.org/inauguration/, accessed 23 June 2014

Imam Siraj Wahhaj

Sister Ayesha Mustafa

Imam Omar Suleiman

Judge Hassan El-Amin

Sister Zahra Billoo

Dr. Altaf Husain

Dr. Ihsan Bagby, who delivered the keynote address, is from the University of Kentucky and a convert to Islam, board member of both ISNA and CAIR, and General Secretary[69] for the Muslim Alliance in North American (MANA). Bagby shared with the audience "a short sojourn through the history of American Muslims starting from the early Africans who were forcibly brought by slave traders to early immigrants to the present. He traced the history of other umbrella organizations that had formed and pointed out the reasons of their demise, urging the council to learn from their mistakes."

As reported by the Muslim Link Paper[70], others in the speaker line-up included **Dr. Ousama Jammal**, Secretary General, USCMO; **Dr. Osama Abu-Irshaid**, Board Member, American Muslims for Palestine; **Nihad Awad**, National Executive Director, Council on American Islamic Relations; **Naeem Baig**, President, Islamic Circle of North America; **Mazen Mokhtar**, Executive Director, Muslim American Society); **Khalil Meek**, Executive Director, Muslim Legal Fund of America; **Imam Delawar Hussein, Dr Lynne Muhammad**[71], Founder, Making A Difference Through Discoveries, American Islamic College, Whitney Young Magnet High School; and **W.D. Mohammed II**, President, Mosque Cares.

USCMO INAUGURAL BANQUET FINANCIAL SPONSORSHIP

The June 2014 USCMO inaugural banquet was sponsored[72] by Helping Hand USA[73] (also known as Helping Hand for Relief and Development), ICNA Relief USA[74], and Guidance Residential[75], the largest U.S. provider of Sharia-compliant home financing. Notably, **the only Muslim charity invited to speak at the formation of the U.S. Council of**

---

[69] Muslim Alliance North America, "MANA'S DIWAN (Executive Committee)," https://www.mana-net.org/subpage.php?ID=about, accessed 23 June 2014

[70] Muslim Link Paper, "New Umbrella Group Holds Inaugural Banquet," http://www.muslimlinkpaper.com/community-news/community-news/3679-new-umbrella-group-holds-inaugural-banquet.html, accessed 23 June 2014

[71] LinkedIn, "Dr. Lynne Muhammad," https://www.linkedin.com/pub/dr-lynne-muhammad/94/1a2/b89?trk=pub-pbmap, accessed 23 June 2014

[72] Muslim Link Paper, "New Umbrella Group Holds Inaugural Banquet," http://www.muslimlinkpaper.com/community-news/community-news/3679-new-umbrella-group-holds-inaugural-banquet.html, accessed 23 June 2014

[73] Helping Hand for Relief and Development, https://www.hhrd.org/ and Helping Hand USA https://www.facebook.com/helpinghandusa, accessed 23 June 2014

[74] ICNA Relief USA, http://icnarelief.org/site2/index.php, accessed 24 June 2014

[75] Guidance Residential, http://www.guidanceresidential.com/about/, accessed 24 June 2014

Muslim Organizations in March 2014 was ICNA's fund, ICNA Relief USA.

Maqsood Ahmad, Executive Director, ICNA Relief USA stated[76] during the banquet that "America is our home and ICNA Relief USA has a goal of making it a better place with Islamic values of compassion, care and giving." Recall that ICNA is the progeny the Muslim Students Association and the jihadist Jamaat-e-Islami movement.

In 2012, ICNA Relief USA received a $30,000 grant from none other than Helping Hand for Relief and Development, a Michigan-based Islamic charity with links to a Pakistani front charity that funds HAMAS. In 2006, the Pakistani charity Al-Khidmat Foundation gave a 6 million rupee check[77] to HAMAS leader Khaled Meshaal[78].

Muslim Brotherhood founder Hassan al-Banna[79], who established the *al-Ikhwan al-Muslimin* in Egypt in 1928 is quoted in the 1988 HAMAS Charter[80] declaring that "Israel will exist and will continue to exist until Islam will obliterate it, just as it obliterated others before it."

The Muslim Link Paper declared that "the [USCMO] banquet was the official introduction for the Muslim community to a platform that promises to open effective communication between Muslim organizations in America and build a national vision."

Imam Omar Ahmad Suleiman, member of ICNA's Shariah Council, represented next generation Muslim Brotherhood leadership in the U.S. and "spoke about what diversity and race relations means to his generation. He expressed great hope for the growth of the council."

---

[76]ICNA Relief USA, "ICNA Relief USA Only Muslim Charity Invited to Speak at Formation of U.S. Council of Muslim Organizations," http://www.icnarelief.org/site2/index.php/blog-post/disaster-relief-efforts/502-icna-relief-usa-only-muslim-charity-invited-to-speak-at-formation-of-u-s-council-of-muslim-organizations, accessed 23 June 2014

[77] Americans Against Hate, http://www.americansagainsthate.org/HamasDonorICNA.htm, accessed 23 June 2014

[78] Steven Emerson, The Investigative Project on Terrorism, IPT News, "Source: Hamas' Meshaal Sets Sights on Brotherhood Post," 27 January 2012. http://www.investigativeproject.org/3413/source-hamas-meshaal-sets-sights-on-brotherhood

[79] Center for Security Policy, Shariah the Threat to America: Report of Team B II, "The Genesis of the Muslim Brotherhood," http://shariahthethreat.org/a-short-course-1-what-is-shariah/a-short-course-9-genesis-of-the-muslim-brotherhood/

[80] Yale School of Law Lillian Goldman Law Library, The Avalon Project, "Hamas Covenant 1988," http://avalon.law.yale.edu/20th_century/hamas.asp

USCMO's Broad Agenda for the American Muslim Community

The USCMO's selection of Zahra Billoo and Altaf Husain as its emcees for the June 2014 inaugural banquet is regrettably notable, especially as USCMO General Secretary Ousama Jammal began the day by introducing "the mission of the council to the audience: bringing American Muslim organizations together." In scope and ambition, this mission appears to be part of the "broad agenda" that Nihad Awad discussed – "In the past, many people have tried to unite on a limited agenda, but this is a broad agenda for the American Muslim community" – when the USCMO officially announced its formation in March 2014.

Broad, indeed, in an anti-American, anti-Semitic agenda if public statements of at least one of its emcees are part of that. Earlier that same day before the USCMO inaugural banquet began, Zahra Billoo, Executive Director of CAIR's San Francisco Chapter, known for her history of publicly-expressed anti-American and anti-Israel sentiment, revealed on Twitter[81] her sympathies for the Taliban, stating that she felt "more responsible for and outraged by US military terrorism in Pakistan than Taliban terrorism there. I fund the former not the latter." Billoo self-describes[82] as an "American, Pakistani, litigious, feminist, hippie, anarchist, outspoken, rebellious, socially conscious Muslimah."

Twitter account for Zahra Billoo, Executive Director of CAIR San Francisco

---

[81] Zahra Billoo's Twitter Account, https://twitter.com/ZahraBilloo, accessed 23 June 2014

[82] Steven Emerson, The Investigative Project on Terrorism, "An IPT Investigative Report: Zahra Billoo," 18 October 2012.
http://www.investigativeproject.org/documents/misc/702.pdf

Although the Islamic Society of North America (ISNA) is not yet an official member of the USCMO, emcee Altaf Husain is a member of ISNA's Majlis Ashura. Husain serves as a faculty member of COMPASS – the Muslim Student Association's state of art management training program; he is also a board member and chair for ISNA's Leadership Development Committee. He was past two-term national president of the Muslim Student Association and an executive committee member of the Muslim Alliance in North America. It is likely only a matter of time before ISNA officially joins forces with the USCMO.

Since the announcement of the USCMO's formation in March 2014, three new Islamic organizations have joined its founding members: **Islamic Shura Council of Southern California, United Muslim Relief, Virginia, and Islamic Center of Wheaton, Illinois. Just over two years ago,** Tariq Ramadan, grandson of Muslim Brotherhood founder Hassan al-Banna, served as a catalyst for action from Muslims in the U.S.

On Sunday, 21 December 2012, Ramadan issued a strong directive to Muslims participating at the 11th Annual MAS-ICNA Convention in Chicago, Illinois, and emboldened the audience when he stated,

> So this is why Muslims when they say we are at home should institutionalize the presence in the country...We are at home, show it! Not show it with what you say, show it with the institutions you have in this country – institutionalize the Muslim presence as Americans. This is home; this is where we can say 'that's where we are'...I think we are reconciling the West with the very essence of our universal principles – if we understand Islam the right way, if we understand why we are experiencing this historical moment of the Muslim presence in the West.

USCMO'S INSTITUTIONALIZED PRESENCE IN THE UNITED STATES

As the USCMO members actively institutionalize their presence, the new coalition of U.S. Muslim organizations would seem to be off to a successful launch, a feat that eluded earlier efforts to unify ideologically-similar but nevertheless discrete American Muslim Brotherhood groups under any sort of political umbrella organization. Previously, in December 1997[83], seven national Islamic organizations had convened unsuccessfully in Sunnyvale, CA to "signify support for the unity process" and provide

---

[83] Washington Report on Middle East Affairs, "SEVEN MUSLIM ORGANIZATIONS ESTABLISH NATIONAL COORDINATION COUNCIL," March 1998. http://www.wrmea.org/wrmea-archives/192-washington-report-archives-1994-1999/march-1998/11744-muslim-american-activism-seven-muslim-organizations-establish-national-coordination-council.html

"coordinated advice to America's six million Muslims on political issues and candidates with creation of a national Coordination Committee." Those organizations at the time included the American Muslim Alliance (AMA), Fremont, CA; American Muslim Caucus (AMC), Dallas, TX; American Muslim Council (AMC), Washington, DC; Council on American-Islamic Relations (CAIR), Washington, DC; National Council on Islamic Affairs, New York City; the Muslim Public Affairs Council (MPAC), Los Angeles; and the Islamic Society of North America (ISNA).

This history of failed efforts by earlier U.S. Muslim organizations to combine efforts and unify leadership for political ends underlines the importance of the current and apparently more successful USCMO initiative. Certainly, the current political climate offers opportunity not previously available to achieve the long-time Brotherhood goal of advancing its civilization jihad plans in accordance with the framework laid out by influential Muslim Brotherhood theoretician Sayyid Qutb in his seminal 1964 monograph 'Milestones.'

While U.S. Muslim organizations have a history of repeated failure to unify their myriad front groups, they have found success in co-opting a narrative of delegitimization, demonization, and victimhood, brazenly stolen from the ranks of those who fight the bigotry of anti-Semitism. This is the "new anti-Semitism" that conflates the genuine Semitism of the Jewish people with the contrived version of their Islamic antagonists. Nothing rallies the Muslim Brotherhood network better, though, than distorting the Jewish experience to its own twisted purposes.

As Natan Sharansky aptly points out, "Anti-Semitism is not a threat only to Jews. History has shown us that left unchecked, the forces behind anti-Semitism will imperil all the values and freedoms that civilization holds dear. Never again can the free world afford to sit on the sidelines when anti-Semitism dangerously emerges. We must not let this happen. We must do everything in our power to fight anti-Semitism. Armed with moral clarity, determination, and a common purpose, this is a fight that we can and will win."[84]

In the early summer of 2014, the U.S. Muslim Brotherhood political party enthusiastically participated in blatantly anti-Semitic demonstrations in downtown Chicago. These protests – and the USCMO leadership's participation in them - are indicative of the true nature of the Muslim Brotherhood and its modus operandi in the U.S. and abroad to wage ideological warfare against Israel and Jews.

---

[84] Natan Sharansky, Jerusalem Center for Public Affairs, "3D Test of Anti-Semitism: Demonization, Double Standards, Delegitimization," *Jewish Political Studies Review 16:3-4*, Fall 2004. http://www.jcpa.org/phas/phas-sharansky-f04.htm

U.S. MUSLIM BROTHERHOOD POLITICAL PARTY PROTESTS AGAINST ISRAEL IN CHICAGO

Anti-Israel protestors in downtown Chicago a block from Israeli Consulate[85]

Around 1,000 Jews and Christians gathered on Tuesday, 22 July 2014 for a mid-day rally to support the nation of Israel outside Metra's Richard B. Ogilvie Transportation Center, the office complex of the Israeli Consulate at 500 W. Madison in downtown Chicago. The U.S. Council of Muslim Organizations (USCMO), the first U.S. Muslim Brotherhood political party, joined in solidarity with approximately 200 pro-Muslim Brotherhood and HAMAS supporters in a counter demonstration at a time of increasing tensions between Muslims and Jews in the Chicago metropolitan area.

---

[85] Photo is property of Center for Security Policy, July 2014

Christians and Jews gather for pro-Israel rally outside Israeli Consulate in Chicago[86]

USCMO SOLIDARITY WITH MUSLIM BROTHERHOOD AND HAMAS

As reported on its Facebook event page, the anti-Israel event Stand with Gaza: Protest Zionism in Chicago![87] held on the 22nd of July was hosted through the US Palestinian Community Network[88], and convened by the Coalition for Justice in Palestine members in the Chicago metropolitan area. The event included participation by the following organizations: American Muslims for Palestine[89], Chicago Islamic Center, Islamic Community Center of Illinois[90], Mosque Foundation[91], Palestinian American Community Center[92], Palestinian American Council[93], Students for Justice in Palestine (SJP)-Chicago[94], and United States Palestinian Community Network[95].

---

[86] Photo is property of Center for Security Policy, July 2014

[87] US Palestinian Community Network Facebook Event page, "Stand with Gaza: Protest Zionism in Chicago!" https://www.facebook.com/events/637353736372609/?ref=51&source=1, accessed 21 July 2014

[88] US Palestinian Community Network Facebook page, https://www.facebook.com/USPCN, accessed 21 July 2014

[89] American Muslims for Palestine, http://www.ampalestine.org/, accessed 21 July 2014

[90] Islamic Community Center of Illinois, http://www.iccionline.com/ICCI_Academy.html, accessed 21 July 2014

[91] Mosque Foundation, http://www.mosquefoundation.org/, accessed 21 July 2014

[92] Palestinian American Community Center, http://www.paccusa.org/, accessed 21 July 2014

[93] Palestinian American Council, http://www.pac-usa.org/, accessed 21 July 2014

[94] Students for Justice in Palestine-Chicago, http://sjpchicago.net/, accessed 21 July 2014

[95] United States Palestinian Community Network, http://uspcn.org/, accessed 21 July 2014

📅 Public · Hosted by US Palestinian Community Network

🕐 Today at 12:00pm
Happening Now · 89°F Mostly Cloudy

📍 500 W. Madison St. Chicago (Across from Israeli Consulate)   Show Map

While millions across the world are rallying in solidarity with the Palestinian people, and for justice in peace in the region, StandWithUs, a right-wing Zionist group is rallying in support of war, occupation, and colonization right here in Chicago.

We won't allow warmongers to gather unopposed in our city, and we are asking everyone to come out and counter protest with us!

Here is the StandWithUs announcement: http://embassies.gov.il/chicago/NewsAndEvents/Pages/A-Rally-to-Stand-Strong-With-Israel.aspx

Convened by the Coalition for Justice in Palestine:

- American Muslims for Palestine (AMP)
- Chicago Islamic Center
- Islamic Community Center of Illinois
- Mosque Foundation
- Palestinian American Community Center
- Palestinian American Council
- Students for Justice in Palestine (SJP)-Chicago
- United States Palestinian Community Network (USPCN)

SPREAD THE WORD. FREE PALESTINE. STAND WITH GAZA.

"Stand with Gaza: Protest Zionism in Chicago"

A highly visible law enforcement presence that included the Chicago Police Department (CPD), CPD SWAT Team, and US DHS police closely guarded the perimeters of the rally to prevent any escalation of violence, as Israel's Operation Protective Edge entered its 15th day destroying HAMAS tunnels in the face of stiff opposition from Palestinian fighters, who continued to lob rockets and missiles into Israel.

As confirmed by CPD News Affairs Officer Jose Estrada in a report from the Chicago Tribune[96] on 20 July, half a dozen cars in Chicago were targeted with anti-Jewish leaflets. These anti-Semitic incidents are now under investigation by the CPD Hate Crime unit. The anti-Jewish leaflets explicitly threatened violence against Jews in Chicago if Israel did not cease its military operations in Gaza.

Anti-Israel demonstrators being contained by Chicago Police Department[97]

The U.S. Council of Muslim Organizations was represented at the anti-Israel event in Chicago notably by the USCMO Secretary General

---

[96] Staff Report, "Anti-Jewish leaflets found on cars on NW Side," *Chicago Tribune*, 20 July 2014. http://www.chicagotribune.com/news/local/breaking/chi-antijewish-leaflets-found-on-cars-on-nw-side-20140720,0,5638885.story

[97] Photo is property of Center for Security Policy, July 2014

Ousama Jammal's Mosque Foundation[98] in Bridgeview, Illinois, where he is currently Vice President. Another USCMO member group, American Muslims for Palestine (AMP), co-founded and chaired by Dr. Hatem Bazian (also the co-founder of Students for Justice in Palestine), showed up as well, carrying AMP posters and signs.

Member participation from the USCMO at the "Stand with Gaza: Protest Zionism in Chicago!" event marks its first public demonstration in solidarity with HAMAS, the Palestinian branch of the Muslim Brotherhood, whose Covenant commits HAMAS to the destruction of the Jewish State of Israel. The USCMO only recently concluded its inaugural banquet together with senior Muslim Brotherhood leadership in June 2014 at a Washington, D.C. venue. Jammal's Mosque Foundation features a troubled history of individuals associated with Muslim Brotherhood front organizations openly supporting HAMAS, a designated Foreign Terrorist Organization.

Jamal Said, current sheikh at the Mosque Foundation, was listed by the Department of Justice as an unindicted co-conspirator in the 2008 Holy Land Foundation (HLF) HAMAS terror funding trial. Several years ago, Said hailed "activists and freedom fighters who gave up their personal ambitions and their own lives so our cause may live.

In a deposition for Boim vs. Quranic Literacy Institute[99], Kifah Mustapha, current sheikh at the Mosque Foundation and active fundraiser for Muslim Brotherhood organizations, was identified as a "registered agent for HLF in Illinois" who raised money for the HLF from the mid-1990s until 2001 when HLF's assets were frozen. Mustapha also served on a Volunteer Committee for the now defunct Islamic Association for Palestine[100] (IAP), a support arm for HAMAS.

Dr. Hatem Bazian, AMP Chairman and frequent guest speaker at Muslim American Society-Islamic Circle of North America Muslim Brotherhood conventions[101], has openly called for an intifada in the United

---

[98] Mosque Foundation Newsletter, July 2014.
http://mosquefoundation.org/images/monthly-newsletters/widget/English_Newsletter_Ramadan_2014.pdf, accessed 23 July 2014
[99] Steven Emerson, The Investigative Project on Terrorism, "Mosque Foundation of Chicago (Bridgeview Mosque) Bridgeview, IL,"
http://www.investigativeproject.org/case/391#_ftn6
[100] Ibid
[101] 13th Annual Muslim American Society-Islamic Circle of North America Convention, "2013 Guest Speakers: Hatem Bazian,"
http://www.masconvention.org/guest-speakers.html, accessed 21 July 2014

States. Bazian once stated: "We're sitting here and watching the world pass by, people being bombed, and it's about time that we have an intifada in this country that change[s] fundamentally the political dynamics in here." He added: 'They're gonna say, 'some Palestinian being too radical' — well, you haven't seen radicalism yet!" At least two current AMP board members[102], Osama Abuirshaid and Salah Sarsour, have ties to HLF[103].

Law enforcement documents confirm that Salah Sarsour helped raise money for HAMAS and formerly worked for the Islamic Association for Palestine (IAP). AMP's Osama Abu Irshaid was an editor of the Arabic newspaper *Al-Zaytounah* published by IAP. Chicago Magistrate Judge Arlander Keys ruled in December 2004 that IAP (and Holy Land Foundation for Relief and Development[104], or HLF), was liable for a $156 million lawsuit[105] for having aided and abetted HAMAS in the West Bank in the killing of David Boim, a 17-year-old American citizen. Thereafter, the U.S. government froze IAP's assets and shut it down on the grounds that it was funding terrorism.

ANTI-SEMITIC CANARDS OF MUSLIM BROTHERHOOD

The AMP is also known for its Islamic anti-Semitism[106] campaign advertisements on mass transportation across the country. Notwithstanding, members of Students for Justice in Palestine, co-founded by Bazian, have terrorized[107] Jewish students with acts of antisemitism on collegiate campuses, while attempting to suppress individuals with pro-Israel views.

---

[102] American Muslims for Palestine, "AMP National Board" http://www.ampalestine.org/index.php/about-amp/amp-national-board, accessed 21 July 2014

[103] Steven Emerson, The Investigative Project on Terrorism, IPT News, "American Muslims for Palestine's Web of Hamas Support," 14 December 2011. http://www.investigativeproject.org/3346/american-muslims-for-palestine-web-of-hamas

[104] Discover the Networks, "Holy Land Foundation for Relief and Development," http://www.discoverthenetworks.org/groupProfile.asp?grpid=6181

[105] The Jewish Community Relations Council of the Jewish United Fund of Metropolitan Chicago, Terrorism Awareness Project, "Chicago Judge and Jury Find Three Local Groups and An Individual Liable for Hamas' Murder of American Teenager; $156 Million Award Set," Spring 2005. http://www.juf.org/pdf/jcrc/tap_spring_2005.pdf

[106] Robert Spencer, Jihad Watch, "AFDI counter anti-Semitic ads from American Muslims for Palestine," 25 March 2014.http://www.jihadwatch.org/2014/03/please-help-afdi-counter-anti-semitic-ads-from-american-muslims-for-palestine

[107] Molly Wharton, "Anti-Semites Rock Colleges," *National Review*, 18 June 2014. http://www.nationalreview.com/article/380695/anti-semites-rock-colleges-molly-wharton

SJP has used its connection with AMP[108] to work more closely to further the goals of HAMAS, and is known for its nationally-coordinated Israel Apartheid Week.[109]

Throughout the course of the anti-Israel counter demonstration on July 22 in Chicago at the southeast corner of Madison and Canal, common themes fomenting anti-Israel, anti-Jewish, and anti-Zionist sentiment were evident among the crowd. The following chants were continuously repeated by the pro-Muslim Brotherhood and HAMAS supporters:

* "Israel, Israel, you cannot hide, we charge you with apartheid."
* "Netanyahu, you cannot hide, we charge you with genocide."
* "Hey Israel, we can see, you are no democracy."
* "Hey Israel, what do you say, how many kids did you kill today?"
* "Hey, hey, ho, ho, the occupation has got to go."
* "Free, free, Palestine, killing children is a crime."
* "We want justice, you saw how? End the siege of Gaza now."

As Jews and Christians gathered peacefully in Chicago to support America's beleaguered ally Israel, the counter-demonstration of pro-Muslim Brotherhood and HAMAS supporters screaming hate-filled invective posed a harsh counterpoint to their quiet prayers and songs.

Since Operation Protective Edge began on 8 July 2014, HAMAS terrorists have fired well over 2,100 rockets and missiles at Israel. In the absence of an agreement to a lasting ceasefire, more anti-Israel demonstrations are planned across the country. Chicago residents braced for more traffic disruptions as pro-Muslim Brotherhood and HAMAS supporters prepared for the 25 July Chicago Day of Al-Quds[110], when they were expected once again to march through the downtown area.

The Center for Security Policy has videos[111] [112] of the anti-Israel demonstrations recording USCMO member involvement in downtown Chicago on 22 July 2014.

---

[108] Lee Kaplan, "Backgrounder: The Students for Justice in Palestine," *Frontpage Magazine*, 17 July 2014. http://www.frontpagemag.com/2014/lee-kaplan/backgrounder-the-students-for-justice-in-palestine/

[109] Caroline Glick, Center for Security Policy, "Are You Proud to be a Leftist?" 10 March 2009. http://www.centerforsecuritypolicy.org/2009/03/10/are-you-proud-to-be-a-leftist-2/

[110] International Day of Al-Quds Facebook page, "Chicago Day of Al-Quds – 2014," https://www.facebook.com/events/1441089229490097/?notif_t=plan_user_invited, accessed 21 July 2014

[111] Secure Freedom YouTube Channel, "Chicago MB Protest 1,"22 July 2014. https://www.youtube.com/watch?v=X7F5q37fPfg

As the USCMO developed its image and expanded its membership to include new Muslim Brotherhood front organizations through the fall of 2014, Secretary General Oussama Jammal and his leadership team became increasingly selective with regard to information provided to the general public about the USCMO's operations and plans. Even as the USCMO carefully released only certain details about its agenda while withholding others, U.S. Congressmen André Carson and Keith Ellison also apparently decided that they would not make available the content of their presentations as keynote speakers at a big June 2014 gala featuring a spread of Muslim Brotherhood-linked organizations pursuing influence operations within the U.S. government.

---

[112] Secure Freedom YouTube Channel, "Chicago MB Protest 2," 22 July 2014. https://www.youtube.com/watch?v=bFVXPvTBfKA

WHY IS USCMO BANQUET FEATURING CONGRESSIONAL MEMBERS STILL SECRET?

Oussama Jammal, Muslim Brotherhood leadership at
10ᵗʰ Annual MAS-ICNA Convention

When the United States commemorated the 13th anniversary of 11 September 2001 and President Barack Obama deliberated a strategy to manage terror threats from the Islamic State (IS), the United States Council of Muslim Organizations (USCMO) and its Secretary General Ousama Jammal still had not published any video, audio, or transcripts from their inaugural banquet held at the Hilton Crystal City Hotel in June 2014. Two current members of Congress, U.S. Representatives Keith Ellison (Democrat, Minnesota's 5th District) and André Carson (Democrat, Indiana's 7th District), were invited by Jammal to speak at the Washington, DC area event which launched the first ever Muslim Brotherhood political party in the U.S. Not even the respective congressional offices have made available publicly the remarks delivered by Ellison and Carson at this high level Muslim Brotherhood function at a time when the Obama administration's foreign policy involving Muslim Brotherhood power-grabs in Egypt, Libya, Syria and elsewhere has been marked by repeated fiascos.

USCMO Secretary General Jammal's Quintessential Leadership Role

USCMO Secretary General Jammal plays a key leadership role for the Muslim Brotherhood's flagship U.S. political party and handles the position of primary spokesman as well. He's well-suited to the Brotherhood messaging agenda: Jammal is president of Fine Media Group, the distribution company for the film *Mohammed: The Last Prophet*, which was completed just months before the 11 September 2001 attacks. The Council on American Islamic Relations (CAIR) praised the film as an opportunity for individuals and families from all faith backgrounds "to learn more about an historic figure like Prophet Mohammed and events that shaped today's world."

In February 2004, Ousama Jammal, then president of the Mosque Foundation in Bridgeview, Illinois characterized the U.S. government counterterrorism program as a "witch hunt." He declared that it was a "Zionist agenda" that prompted federal officials to close three Islamic charities operating near the mosque and prevent Sabri Samirah, a leader from the mosque and Chairman of the Board of Directors for the Islamic Association for Palestine (IAP), from returning to the U.S. from Jordan. What Jammal neglected to mention was that, in fact, it was a HAMAS operative – Mousa Abu Marzook – who established the Islamic Association for Palestine in 1981. On 8 October 1987, the U.S. Department of State (DoS) designated HAMAS a Foreign Terrorist Organization (FTO). The IAP was also parent to the Council on American Islamic Relations, which was incorporated in 1994 by the IAP leadership that included Nihad Awad (current CAIR National Executive Director and USCMO member), Omar Ahmad, and Rafeeq Jaber.

As shown by court documents, the IAP was a prong of the Muslim Brotherhood's Palestine Committee, until the U.S. government froze the IAP's assets and shut it down in December 2004 on the grounds that it was funding terrorism. The IAP was identified as one of the Muslim Brotherhood's twenty-nine likeminded "organizations of our friends" in the May 1991 Muslim Brotherhood document "An Explanatory Memorandum on the General Strategic Goal for the Group in North America."

CONGRESSMEN KEITH ELLISON, ANDRÉ CARSON MOBILIZE THE MUSLIM POLITICAL MACHINE

Before USCMO Secretary General Jammal invited U.S. Representatives Ellison and Carson to the USCMO's historic inaugural event in June 2014 in the Washington, DC area, he likely would have been aware that both these members of Congress previously had participated at various conventions of Muslim Brotherhood organizations. One of these engagements included the Islamic Society of North America's annual convention in August 2008, where Ellison and Carson discussed effective strategies for the community-based political advocacy necessary to mobilize the Muslim political machine in the U.S.

In December 2008, U.S. Representative Ellison made history as the first member of Congress to make a MAS-sponsored hajj pilgrimage to Mecca. The Muslim American Society (MAS) was created by the Muslim Brotherhood; MAS also is a founding member of the USCMO. In 2007 and 2008, Ellison gave the keynote address at MAS conventions in Minnesota.[113] This very same MAS Minnesota chapter that paid for Ellison's hajj highlighted writings on its website from Islamic clerics who praised HAMAS and urged Muslims to "wage Jihad until death."[114] The architects of HAMAS and some of Al-Qaeda's founding figures were members of the Muslim Brotherhood first.

During a Muslim American Society-Islamic Circle of North America (MAS-ICNA) convention in the summer of 2012, U.S. Representative Carson stated in his address about the *State of The American Family* that "America will never win the war against terrorism without help from the Muslim community. America will never tap into educational innovation and ingenuity without looking at the model that we have in our madrassas, in our schools, where innovation is encouraged, where the foundation is the Quran."[115] [116]

---

[113] Joseph Abrams, "Group That Funded Rep. Ellison's Pilgrimage to Mecca Called a Front for Extremism," *Fox News*, 8 January 2009. http://www.foxnews.com/politics/2009/01/08/group-funded-rep-ellisons-pilgrimage-mecca-called-extremism/

[114] Ibid

[115] Islamic Circle of North America YouTube Channel, "ICNA-MAS 2012: The State of The American Family by Congressman Andre Carson," https://www.youtube.com/watch?v=4A8NMhqAw1M&list=PLumLWdoAMX1d1 GfT8dQ2A3JJf55aIzSke&index=7, accessed 5 September 2014

[116] David Martosko, "Democrats will appoint Muslim to the House Intelligence Committee who said US schools should be like Islamic madrassas and warned law enforcement that 'Allah will not allow you to stop us'," *Daily Mail*, 14 January

Carson continued on an aggrieved and somewhat exaggerate theme, noting that "America must understand that she needs Muslims. There are over 7 million Muslims in this country. While we are under attack, we cannot retreat. We have been a part of America since the inception of America...Now, It is unfortunate that there are those who are thinking at this convention right now, we are having secret meetings, that we are plotting to destroy this country. But I say to those who are here undercover, Allah will not allow you to stop us."[117] [118]

The lack of transparency apparently favored by the USCMO and its Secretary General Jammal, at least when U.S. Congressmen with a record of Muslim Brotherhood linkages are involved, doesn't bode well for any of them. Careful control of the USCMO image, narrative, and messaging to the U.S. public may shield them from criticism for the moment, but at a time when the Muslim Brotherhood has been declared a terrorist entity by Egypt, Saudi Arabia, and the United Arab Emirates, and the Islamic State (a similarly jihadist organization) is running amok across the Middle East, it is going to be difficult for the USCMO—or its Congressional alliances—to maintain the facade forever.

2015. http://www.dailymail.co.uk/news/article-2910327/Democrats-appoint-Muslim-House-Intelligence-Committee-said-schools-like-Islamic-madrassas-warned-law-enforcement-Allah-not-allow-stop-us.html

[117] Ibid

[118] See Center for Security Policy's special report on Congressman Andre Carson: "Center Releases Dossier Documenting a House Intelligence Committee Member's Extensive Ties to the Muslim Brotherhood," 24 February 2015. http://www.centerforsecuritypolicy.org/2015/02/24/center-releases-dossier-documenting-a-house-intelligence-committee-members-extensive-ties-to-the-muslim-brotherhood/

U.S. COUNCIL OF MUSLIM ORGANIZATIONS RAISES FUNDS FOR ISLAMIC RELIEF USA

The newly-formed U.S. Muslim Brotherhood political party, the U.S. Council of the Muslim Organizations (USCMO), has lost no time diving into the American political scene during the 2014 election year, surrounded by well-known individuals and groups that sport long histories of Brotherhood associations. On 6 September 2014, USCMO member organizations gathered in Rosemont, Illinois for a fundraising event hosted by Islamic Relief USA (IRUSA) and a dinner sponsored by the Chicago Islamic Organizations of Greater Chicago (CIGOC).[119] As the largest Muslim charity in this country, IRUSA was incorporated in California in 1993 as a 501c3 tax exempt charity. IRUSA has a troubling history that includes providing financial assistance to the Florida branch of CAIR (Council on American Islamic Relations).

CAIR, of course, is well-known for its own Brotherhood and HAMAS pedigree. In 2008, CAIR was named an unindicted co-conspirator by the Department of Justice in the Holy Land Foundation (HLF) HAMAS terror funding trial. Following a 108-count unanimous guilty verdict, the HLF was put out of business; its Muslim Brotherhood leadership was sentenced to lengthy terms in federal prison. IRUSA's United Kingdom-based parent organization, Islamic Relief Worldwide (IRW), was established in 1984 and also has Muslim Brotherhood connections.

American Muslim Brotherhood Leadership Figures Participate at Islamic Relief USA Fundraiser

The IRUSA fundraiser was held at the Donald E. Stephens Convention Center, a site used for a number of years to hold international conventions organized by prominent Muslim Brotherhood groups including the Islamic Society of North America (ISNA) and Islamic Circle of North America (ICNA). Keynote addresses were delivered that evening by Karen Koning Abuzayd, Assistant Secretary General of the United Nations Relief and Works Agency for Palestine Refugees (UNRWA) and Sheikh Imam Jamal Said from the Mosque Foundation in Bridgeview, Illinois.

---

[119] Islamic Relief USA, "Chicago, IL: Fundraising Dinner for Palestine," http://www.irusa.org/events/chicago-il-fundraising-dinner-for-palestine/, accessed 5 September 2014

Jamal Said is listed as a member of the Muslim Brotherhood offshoot called the Palestine Section in the 1993 By-Laws of the Palestine Committee, parent organization of the Islamic Association for Palestine (itself the parent organization of CAIR). Said also appeared on the Department of Justice (DOJ) Attachment A list of unindicted co-conspirators in a section for Palestine Committee members as part of the evidence presented at the United States of America vs. Holy Land Foundation for Relief and Development HAMAS terror funding trial of 2008. His name also appears on an internal Palestine Committee telephone list obtained by the DOJ prosecutors. As shown in the screenshot below, IRUSA promoted this event as a "Fundraising Dinner for Palestine" on its website.

Islamic Relief USA: Chicago "Fundraising Dinner for Palestine"

Participation120 by American Muslim Brotherhood leadership at the Islamic Relief USA fundraiser on 6 September 2014 included USCMO Secretary General Oussama Jammal's Mosque Foundation and USCMO members Muslim American Society (MAS), American Muslims for Palestine (AMP), Islamic Circle of North America, and the Islamic Center of Wheaton. The following advertisement121 for this IRUSA fundraiser

---

[120] The Council of Islamic Organizations of Greater Chicago, "Relief USA to host fundraising dinner for Palestine on September 6," 4 September 2014 http://www.ciogc.org/index.php/mediarelations/articles-and-statements/468-9-4-14-islamic-relief-usa-to-host-fundraising-dinner-for-palestine-on-september-6, accessed 5 September 2014

[121] Ibid

appeared on the website for the Chicago Islamic Organizations of Greater Chicago.

Islamic Relief USA: advertisement for September 2014 fundraising event

The IRUSA has also been able to promote itself as the recipient of a presidential endorsement: during the National Prayer Breakfast[122] on 2 February 2012, President Barack Obama openly praised the work of IRUSA. In the following screenshot from its website, the IRUSA posts that "During his speech at the 2012 National Prayer Breakfast, President Barak Obama cited IRUSA as one of the faith-based organizations helping bring hope to those suffering around the world."

IRUSA noting recognition of its work by US President Barack Obama

Less than 4 months before that National Prayer Breakfast, IRUSA was one of 57 organizations joined by CAIR, ICNA, and MAS (all current USCMO members) to co-sign a letter[123] on 19 October 2011 authored by Farhana Khera, Executive Director for Muslim Advocates. Khera wrote to President Barack Obama's Deputy National Security Advisor for Homeland Security and Counterterrorism (and future Central Intelligence Agency Director) John Brennan, urging him to take action over US government training materials alleged to demonstrate a prejudice against Islam. Subsequently, in August 2014, not satisfied with the ensuing government-

---

[122] The White House, Office of the Press Secretary, "Remarks by the President at the National Prayer Breakfast," 2 February 2012. http://www.whitehouse.gov/the-press-office/2012/02/02/remarks-president-national-prayer-breakfast

[123] "Robert Spencer, "The Human Cost of Jihad Denial," *Frontpage Magazine*, 2 May 2013. http://frontpagemag.com/2013/robert-spencer/the-human-cost-of-jihad-denial/

wide purge of all curriculum materials that taught the inspirational linkage between Islamic doctrine and Islamic terrorism, signatories of the October 2011 letter (but not including IRUSA) sent a new letter[124] to Lisa Monaco, Brennan's successor, urging the Obama administration to "Implement a mandatory retraining program for all federal, state and local law enforcement officials who have been subjected to biased and discriminatory trainings provided by the federal government."

ISLAMIC RELIEF USA'S PURPORTED MISSION AS A CHARITY

And yet, on its website, IRUSA purports[125] to be a charitable agency that "strives to alleviate suffering, hunger, illiteracy, and diseases worldwide regardless of color, race, religion, or creed, and to provide aid in a compassionate and dignified manner. Islamic Relief USA aims to provide rapid relief in the event of human and natural disasters and to establish sustainable local development projects allowing communities to better help themselves."

Apparently the apple doesn't fall far from the tree. In a May 2006 statement[126] from Israeli Prime Minister Ehud Olmert's Office concerning the arrest of a Pakistani-born British national and IRW Gaza branch project director, the Israeli Ministry of Foreign Affairs noted that "The IRW provides support and assistance to HAMAS's infrastructure. The IRW's activities in Judea, Samaria and the Gaza Strip are carried out by social welfare organizations controlled and staffed by HAMAS operatives. The intensive activities of these associations are designed to further HAMAS's ideology among the Palestinian population."

The following Facebook screenshot photo is of some significance due to a notable guest at the IRUSA fundraiser in September 2014. Pictured second from the right is Sabri Samirah, described by the newspaper Al

---

[124] Muslim Advocates, Letter to Lisa O. Monaco Assistant to the President for Homeland Security and Counterterrorism, 14 August 2014. http://www.muslimadvocates.org/files/FINALCoalitionLetterTrainings_8.14.14.pdf

[125] Islamic Relief USA, "About Us," http://www.irusa.org/islamic-relief-usa/, accessed 5 September 2014

[126] Israeli Ministry of Foreign Affairs, Communicated by the Prime Minister's Office, "British national arrested for assisting Hamas," 29 May 2006. http://www.mfa.gov.il/mfa/foreignpolicy/terrorism/palestinian/pages/british%20national%20arrested%20for%20assisting%20hamas%2029-may-2006.aspx

Jazeera[127] as "a political analyst and leading member of the Muslim Brotherhood in Jordan."

Sabri Samirah (second from right) at Islamic Relief USA fundraiser

Sabri Samirah, former chairman[128] of the Islamic Association for Palestine[129] in North America (IAP), a direct HAMAS[130] off-shoot and the parent organization of CAIR, returned to Chicago, Illinois in 2014 after 11 years in exile. Samirah has a history of associations with Muslim Brotherhood leaders calling for the annihilation of worldwide Jewry and the nation of Israel. Following the events of 11 September 2001, Samirah was prohibited[131] by the U.S. Department of State in 2003 from entering this

---

[127] "Unrest in Jordan: What does the future hold for the Jordanian government and the king who appointed it?" *Al Jazeera*, 28 March 2011.
http://www.aljazeera.com/programmes/insidestory/2011/03/201132892612534426.html

[128] The Investigative Project on Terrorism, Islamic Association for Palestine 4th Annual Convention: "All Palestine Is Sacred," 23-25 November 2000.
http://www.investigativeproject.org/documents/misc/438.pdf

[129] The Investigative Project on Terrorism, "Islamic Action for Palestine - An internal memo," October 1992.
http://www.investigativeproject.org/documents/misc/23.pdf#page=14

[130] The Investigative Project on Terrorism, "Terrorist Organizations and Other Groups of Concern: Hamas (Updated August 24, 2007)," "Chapter 8: Foreign Terrorist Organizations," Country Reports on Terrorism 2005, US Department of State, April 30, 2006 http://www.investigativeproject.org/profile/129

[131] Leagle, Inc., SAMIRAH v. O'CONNELL No. 03-1786. 335 F.3d 545 (2003)
http://www.leagle.com/decision/2003880335F3d545_1824.xml/SAMIRAH%20v.%20O%27CONNELL

country because the "District Director of the Chicago INS Office, acting on behalf of the Attorney General, revoked his advance parole because the INS had received information that he was a 'security risk to the United States.'"

As alluded to above, an IRUSA Form 990 2013 tax return[132] filed in July 2014 revealed that CAIR's Florida branch was the recipient of $45,495 in grants from IRUSA. The IRUSA also gave $40,000 to the Dar Al-Hijrah Islamic Center in Falls Church Virginia, where senior Al-Qaeda leader Anwar al-Awlaki[133] was imam during the timeframe leading up to events of September 11, 2001 and immediately thereafter.

That prominent USCMO members stand in solidarity with IRUSA is not coincidental given their members' participation at the "Stand with Gaza: Protest Zionism in Chicago!" event toward the end of July 2014. That marked the USCMO's first public demonstration in solidarity with HAMAS, the Palestinian branch of the Muslim Brotherhood, whose Covenant commits HAMAS to the destruction of the Jewish State of Israel.

While Prime Minister Benjamin Netanyahu's Defense Minister Moshe Ya'alon issued[134] a ruling in June 2014 to ban IRW operations anywhere in Israel, Judea, and Samaria and to prohibit the transfer of funds by IRW to Judea and Samaria, IRUSA was in the planning stages for another fundraiser in the Chicago area. IRUSA advertised its "Fundraising Dinner for Gaza"[135] which was held on 8 November 2014 in Oak Brook, Illinois just after the U.S. midterm elections.

[132] IR USA, 2013 Form 990 Return, http://www.irusa.org/content/uploads/2014/08/IRUSA-2013-Form-990-Pub-Insp-Copy.pdf, accessed 2 October 2014

[133] Steven Emerson, The Investigative Project on Terrorism, "Dar Al-Hijrah Official's Deception on Awlaki," 18 November 2009. http://www.investigativeproject.org/1521/dar-al-hijrah-officials-deception-on-awlaki

[134] JPost Staff, "Israel bans Islamic Relief Worldwide from West Bank due to Hamas ties," Jerusalem Post, 19 June 2014. http://www.jpost.com/Operation-Brothers-Keeper/Israel-bans-Islamic-Relief-Worldwide-from-West-Bank-due-to-Hamas-ties-359934

[135] Islamic Relief USA, "Oak Brook, IL: Fundraising Dinner for Gaza," http://www.irusa.org/events/oak-brook-il-fundraising-dinner-for-gaza/, accessed 20 October 2014

Islamic Relief USA: Oak Brook November 2014 "Fundraising Dinner for Gaza"

The USCMO's growing network of Brotherhood-linked affiliations, especially those like IRUSA with such direct links to Middle Eastern terrorism, marks this political party as a group to watch. As political activity began to ramp up through the November 2014 congressional elections and beyond, to the U.S. presidential elections of 2016, this Muslim Brotherhood coalition appeared poised to expand its circle of influence across the U.S. political scene.

In 2014, Jordanian Muslim Brotherhood leader Sabri Samirah, previously banned from the United States for a decade, returned to the U.S. and quickly began to turn his understanding of the American political process to the tasking of the USCMO political agenda. Throughout 2014, Samirah worked with Secretary General Jammal and USCMO leadership to prepare a roadmap for implementing that agenda.

A VETERAN BROTHER EMERGES TO LEAD THE USCMO POLITICAL AGENDA

The U.S. Council of Muslim Organizations used the November 2014 midterm elections to advance a number of its operational objectives through mobilization of Muslim voters in Illinois. Sabri Samirah, a political analyst and leading member of the Muslim Brotherhood in Jordan, led USCMO efforts to "get out the vote" in Illinois. As will be recalled, Samirah, former chairman of the Islamic Association for Palestine (IAP) in North America, a direct HAMAS off-shoot and the parent organization of CAIR (Council on American Islamic Relations), returned to Chicago, Illinois earlier in 2014 after 11 years in exile abroad. Samirah, no stranger to the Illinois political arena, quickly assumed leadership of several organizations.

REINVENTION OF BANNED JORDANIAN MUSLIM BROTHERHOOD LEADER

He is President of the newly-established American and Middle Eastern Affairs Center Think Tank[136] (AMEAC) and CEO of the Development Institute for Consultation & Training, LLC, and (DICT).[137] Prior to his 2003 deportation from the United States, Samirah previously had served as President of United Muslim Americans Association (UMAA) from 1999-2003. Now, playing on the same theme of Muslim unity, as Executive Director, he also heads another new organization called "UMMA" (not an acronym but the full name), established in September 2014 with its forthcoming website at www.OurUMMA.org.

Both of these organizations, described in more detail in the following chapters, played a role in the 2014 USCMO voter mobilization campaign and appeared to be positioning themselves to expanding that role further in the lead-up to the 2016 presidential elections. USCMO members actively helped coordinate a campaign to endorse statewide and federal political candidates viewed as accommodating toward Islam and Shariah,

---

[136] Sabri Samirah, Facebook page, "American and Middle Eastern Affairs Think Tank," https://www.facebook.com/AMEACThinkTank, accessed 20 August 2014
[137] Sabri Samirah, LinkedIn Account, "Development Institute for Consultation & Training, LLC, (DICT)," http://www.linkedin.com/in/sabrisamirah, accessed 20 August 2014

including Illinois Republican Governor-elect, Bruce Rauner (who was inaugurated on 12 January 2015). This chapter will highlight the emerging leadership role being played within the USCMO by Sabri Samirah.

While he is self-described as a "moderate, modern, Muslim, Arab American thinker[138];" Samirah has a history of associations with Muslim Brotherhood leaders who have called for the annihilation of worldwide Jewry and the nation of Israel. In 2003, the U.S. Department of State prohibited[139] Samirah from entering this country within the scope of security measures implemented after the attacks of 11 September 2001. Officially, the "District Director of the Chicago INS Office, acting on behalf of the Attorney General, revoked his advance parole because the INS had received information that he was a 'security risk to the United States.'" None of this prior background, however, deterred U.S. officials in 2014 from allowing him to return to the country, once again to take a key leadership position among Brotherhood-affiliated groups with a presence in Illinois and across the United States.

Just weeks after returning to the U.S., Samirah was a speaker at a 5 April 2014 fundraising dinner held by USCMO member group, the American Muslims for Palestine (AMP). He was introduced[140] as "a longtime global and national Palestinian activist." Another role model singled out for praise at the event was Rasmieh Odeh[141], a convicted terrorist who spent ten years in an Israeli prison. At this AMP dinner, she was praised by master of ceremonies Rami Bleibel as "a great community member, a great member for the Palestinian cause." Later, in November 2014, Odeh would be found guilty of illegally entering the U.S. in 1995 for failure to disclose her prior terrorist record in Israel. Following her October 2013 indictment, Odeh was charged with naturalization fraud and eventually found guilty in the federal court case *USA v. Odeh, Rasmieh Yousef* of illegally

---

[138] Sabri Samirah Facebook page, "Dr. Sabri Samirah Page in English: Info," https://www.facebook.com/DrSabriSamirahPageInEnglishUsAmerica/info, accessed 21 August 2014

[139] Leagle, Inc., SAMIRAH v. O'CONNELL No. 03-1786. 335 F.3d 545 (2003) http://www.leagle.com/decision/2003880335F3d545_1824.xml/SAMIRAH%20v.%20O%27CONNELL

[140] Steven Emerson, The Investigative Project on Terrorism, "IPT Exclusive: AMP's Telling Choice of Heroes," 8 April 2014. http://www.investigativeproject.org/4346/ipt-exclusive-amp-telling-choice-of-heroes

[141] Steven Emerson, The Investigative Project on Terrorism, "USA v. Odeh, Rasmieh Yousef: Popular Front for the Liberation of Palestine (PFLP)," Updated March 2015. http://www.investigativeproject.org/case/652

entering the U.S. in 1995, when she did not disclose either her PFLP affiliation or her conviction and prison time in Israel in paperwork filed with U.S. immigration authorities.

The following picture is a screenshot of Samirah's Facebook page, showing him at the speaker's podium during the April 2014 AMP gathering of Muslim Brotherhood leadership.

Sabri Samriah addressing Muslim Brotherhood at AMP fundraising dinner

SABRI SAMIRAH LEADS MUSLIM BROTHERHOOD IN ANTI-ISRAEL DEMONSTRATIONS IN CHICAGO

One month later, during a May 2014 interview[142] with the *Chicago Tribune*, Samirah expressed his desire for a lower profile in the U.S. His highly visible, proactive leadership at July 2014 anti-Israel demonstrations with thousands of HAMAS and Muslim Brotherhood supporters in downtown Chicago would seem to indicate otherwise, as would his eventual emergence in top leadership positions of a clutch of Brotherhood-affiliated organizations. USCMO member organizations and Samirah himself figured prominently in protests[143] organized for 5 July 2014 in response to initial Israeli actions that followed a finding of HAMAS responsibility for the kidnapping and murder of three Israeli teens. Operation Protective Edge, that galvanized a further wave of protests, was launched on 8 July. As photos[144] on his own Facebook page show, Samirah was an active participant in those early anti-Israel demonstrations in downtown Chicago[145]. The following screenshot is from his Facebook account on 6 July 2014.

---

[142] Allison Hantschel, "Muslim activist returns to suburbs after decade in exile," *Chicago Tribune*, 25 May 2014. http://articles.chicagotribune.com/2014-05-25/news/ct-exiled-muslim-returns-met-20140525_1_sima-srouri-sabri-samirah-security-risk

[143] SJP Chicago Facebook, "Protest against Israel's collective punishment on Gaza and West Bank and its violence against Palestinian youth," https://www.facebook.com/events/1479409155627269/, accessed, 3 July 2014

[144] Sabri Samirah Facebook page, "Rally for Palestine, at Chicago," https://www.facebook.com/Sabri.Samirah/posts/10152599728732433, accessed 9 July 2014

[145] Gregory Pratt, "Protesters blast Israeli military action, media," *Chicago Tribune*, 5 July 2014. http://www.chicagotribune.com/news/local/breaking/chi-protesters-blast-israeli-military-action-media-20140705-story.html

Sabri Samirah at Rally for Palestine in Chicago

He even praised[146] Ahmed Rehab (Chicago Executive Director, Council on American Islamic Relations) as "brilliant" on 16 July 2014 for his mockery of U.S. citizens deemed ignorant by Rehab for their support of Israel.

 Sabri Samirah via **Ahmed Rehab**
July 16 · 🌐

Brilliant Ahmed Rehab. Being brainwashed about Palestine. Please, read the full text. Thanks Ahmed.
+ + + + + + + + + +

Sabri Samirah demonstrates support for CAIR Chicago Executive Director Ahmed Rehab

A week later, Samirah made the following post to on his Facebook page demanding action to stop military aid to Israel, including amounts included in the 2015 U.S. Department of Defense Appropriations Act.[147]

---

[146] Sabri Samirah Facebook page,
https://www.facebook.com/Sabri.Samirah/posts/10152599728732433, accessed 10 November 2014

[147] Sabri Samirah Facebook page,
https://www.facebook.com/Sabri.Samirah/posts/10152599728732433, accessed 10 November 2014

Sabri Samirah supports petition to stop 2015 U.S. Department of Defense Appropriations Act

Despite his absence from the United States for 11 years, Samirah's speech on 26 July 2014 in downtown Chicago did not miss a beat in "advancing Justice for Palestine and the Palestinian people" when he addressed thousands of pro-HAMAS and Muslim Brotherhood supporters in the streets. The following photo of Samirah speaking was posted online and depicts him rallying the demonstrators; this also references a video of him that afternoon in Chicago. [148]

---

[148] Secure Freedom YouTube Channel, "Sabri Samirah at Chicago Rally for Palestine," 26 July 2014. https://www.youtube.com/watch?v=AYQUCltAyUU

Muslim Brotherhood "Grassroots Unified Voting Bloc" Election Strategy

As shown in the following screenshot from his Facebook page on 27 July 2014, Samirah already was moving from grassroots organization to strategizing about how to mobilize voters in advance of the November 2014 midterm elections. To this end, he urged formation of a "Grassroots Unified Voting Bloc" that would energize Muslim voters to unify and collectively think and work on participating in those elections. As would become increasingly evident shortly, the Gaza and Palestinian focus was only an initial wedge issue – and the USCMO had its sights set on a much broader political spectrum than that.

Sabri Samirah
July 27 · Edited · 📷

For English, keep reading at "see more" below.

رئيس مركز الشؤون الأمريكية والشرق أوسطية (مركز تفكير)، د. صبري سميرة، متحدثاً في مسيرة هي الأضخم في شيكاغو نصرة لغزة وفلسطين يحث الجالية على التوحد والتفكير والعمل الجماعيين للمشاركة في الإنتخابات الأمريكية في شهر نوفمبر وخلق "مجموعة تصويت موحدة شعبية" لتحقيق تقوية سياسية وعامة تساعدهم في خدمة قضاياهم بأثواعها بما في ذلك قضية غزة وفلسطين

AMEAC's President, Dr. Sabri Samirah, speaking at a biggest rally for Gaza & Palestine in Chicago, demands the community to, unify and collectively, think and work on participating in Nov. American elections and create a " Grassroots Unified Voting Bloc" to achieve public & political empowerment in order to serve their issues everywhere including in Gaza & Palestine.
#ChicagostandswithGaza #AJAGAZA #FreeGaza #FreePalestine #ISupportGaza #GazaUnderAttack #GazaUnderFire #Gaza

See Translation

140726 Chicago Rally for Palestine.AVI

Shared with Dropbox

DROPBOX.COM

Like · Comment · Share

👍 19 people like this.

Sabri Samirah at Rally for Palestine in Chicago in July 2014

Indicative of his goal to reach a broader American electorate, and already having achieved a measure of success with the participation by Jews and Christians who also took to Chicago streets to protest Israel's Operation Protective Edge, Samirah noted in a Facebook letter[149] posted on 31 July 2014 that "I should not remind you of how constructive our status would be if, we have a real public and political influence in serving our causes in America and around the globe; i.e. the catastrophe, now, in Gaza."

SAMIRAH: CONDUIT FOR USCMO OPERATIONS

The new USCMO member Islamic Center of Wheaton, IL invited Samirah to deliver a Friday afternoon *khutba* or sermon on 1 August 2014. The following screenshot is a post made by Samirah on Facebook, where he is leading the *khutba* on the 1st of August at Islamic Center of Wheaton.

Sabri Samirah leading Friday Khutba at the Islamic Center in Wheaton, Illinois

---

[149] Sabri Samirah Facebook page, https://www.facebook.com/Sabri.Samirah/posts/10152599728732433, accessed 10 November 2014

Their selection of Samirah was not a surprise, as he had previously solidified a relationship with their leadership. As shown in the screenshot below from his Facebook page, he had been at the Islamic Center of Wheaton in March 2014 along with leadership from the Council of Islamic Organizations of Greater Chicago (CIOG) to help fundraise for the newly-opened Center.

Sabri Samirah & CIGOC Chairman at fundraising dinner for
USCMO Member Islamic Center of Wheaton

The Islamic Center of Wheaton would officially join the USCMO in the early summer of 2014. Prior to December of 2013, this property purchased by the Islamic Center of Wheaton, formerly was a Christian church named the First Assembly of God, as shown in the following picture.

*Former First Assembly of God Church, home to USCMO Member
Islamic Center of Wheaton*[150]

The next picture shows a sign that currently greets passersby traveling through this heavily trafficked area.

Marquee for Islamic Center of Wheaton[151]

Also prior to his August 2014 Friday sermon at the Wheaton Islamic Center, Samirah delivered a *khutba* on 12 July 2014 at the Islamic Center in Claremont, California—another community concerned about

---

[150] Photo is property of Center for Security Policy, July 2014

[151] Photo is property of Center for Security Policy, July 2014

perceptions that Islam may be linked to Islamic terrorism. In a November 2012 news report[152], Islamic centers leaders were asked to respond to the fact that three of the four men accused of planning a terrorist attack on U.S. military bases in Afghanistan were from Riverside, Pomona, and Upland. When Sam Badwan, the chairman of the board of directors of the Islamic Center of Claremont in Pomona, was interviewed about this, he expressed concern "that whenever anyone is arrested who claims to be planning terrorist attacks in the name of Islam, **he and other Muslims always worry that misunderstandings of Islam will spread.**"

The following screenshot is from Samirah's Facebook page where he describes his activities as "Friday Khutba & Prayer, Taraweeh, and Fundraising for the Center."

---

[152] Robert Spencer, Jihad Watch, "Relax: Southern California Muslim leaders say arrested jihadis don't represent Islam," 20 November 2012. http://www.jihadwatch.org/2012/11/relax-southern-california-muslim-leaders-say-arrested-jihadis-dont-represent-islam

Sabri Samirah added 8 new photos to the album جمعة مركز
Friday of Is. Center of Claremont, CA كليرموت الاسلامي.
July 12

Friday Khutba & Prayer, Taraweeh, and Fundraising for the Center.
خطبة وصلاة الجمعة والتراويح وجمع تبرعات لصالح المركز الاسلامي — in Claremont,
California.

Like Comment Share

53 people like this.

"Friday Khutba & Prayer, Taraweeh, and Fundraising" for
Islamic Center of Claremont, CA

As reported by The Muslim Observer on 12 August 2014, Samirah joined nationally and internationally recognized leadership and organizations of the Muslim Brotherhood as a signatory to the "End Israeli Aggression

74

and Occupation[153]" statement under his newly established think tank, the American and Middle Eastern Affairs Center (AMEAC). The following screenshot is from The Muslim Observer website highlighting several of these organizations that Samirah joined in solidarity.

Signatures

A. Organizations

American Muslims for Palestine (AMP)
American Muslim Alliance (AMA)
Council on American-Islamic Relations (CAIR)
Islamic Circle of North America (ICNA)
Muslim American Society (MAS)
Northern California Islamic Council (NCIC)
Pakistan American Democratic Forum (PADF)
Peace Thru Justice Foundation (PTJF)
Muslim Voters of America (MVA)
Muslim American Society (MAS)
Muslim Ummah of North America (MUNA)
Muslim Public Affairs Council (MPAC)
Islamic Circle of North America (ICNA)
Palestinian American Society (PAS)
Shura Council Southern California

American and Middle Eastern Affairs Center (AMEAC Think Ta

IQRAâ€™ International Educational Foundation
IslamiCity
American Muslim Voice
Arab Muslim American Federation
Muslim Progressive Traditionalist Alliance
Lamppost Productions
Muslim Navayath Voice
Muslim Peace Fellowship
Sahaba Initiative

AMEAC Think Tank Signatory on "End Israeli Aggression and Occupation" statement

---

[153] The Muslim Observer, "Statement "End Israeli Aggression and Occupation"," 12 August 2014. http://muslimmedianetwork.com/mmn/?p=15951, accessed 18 August 2014

Samirah was also a speaker at the USCMO member Islamic Circle of North America's Midwest convention "Islam: Faith, Submission, Service" held on 15-17 August 2014 in Peoria, Illinois. The following is a screenshot of Samirah from his Facebook page showing him speaking at the podium during a main session about "Muslims around the World Series I: Egypt & Palestine: Where to?"

Sabri Samirah addressing Muslim Brotherhood at 2014 ICNA Midwest Convention

At the end of August 2014, Samirah traveled to Milwaukee, Wisconsin where he addressed Muslim Brotherhood supporters at the "Celebrating the Steadfastness of Gaza" event sponsored by USCMO member American Muslims for Palestine (AMP).

Sabri Samirah added 6 new photos to the album Sumood
Gaza, Milwaukee, WI Aug 29, 2014.
August 30 ·

I was honored to speak at the event. تشرفت بأن ألقيت كلمة في المناسبة
Steadfastness of Gaza : See Below

احتفالية صمود غزة في المركز الاسلامي في مدينة ميلواكي , ولاية ويسكونسن في الولايات المتحدة الامريكية

شارك المئات من العرب والمسلمين وانصارهم من غير المسلمين في احياء أمسية " احتفالية صمود غزة" وقدم العديد من القيادات كلمات الدعم والتأييد لغزة وصمودها

Hundred of Muslims and non Muslims in Milwaukee, Wisconsin, gathered
for " Celebrating the Steadfastness of Gaza. Many leaders spoke in
support of Gaza and its people including a speech by the spokeswoman o
the group Friends of Palestine — with Salah Sarsour and Ziad Hamdan.

Like · Comment · Share

AMP "Celebrating Steadfast of Gaza"

These various examples of Samirah's active leadership in Illinois and throughout the U.S. over the course of a few short months in 2014 suggest rather strongly that Samirah has been selected by top levels of the international Brotherhood leadership to help catalyze the next steps of Civilization Jihad described in its 1991 document "An Explanatory Memorandum on the General Strategic Goal for the Group in North America." It would seem, however, that that role, however well-received among the U.S. *Ikhwan* network, was not necessarily intended to be highlighted more publicly outside of it.

Samirah may in fact be a bit more publicity-shy than generally thought: sometime towards late December 2014 or early January 2015, his three different Facebook accounts **Sabri Samirah, Dr. Sabri Samirah Page / in English / US America**, and **American Middle-Eastern Affairs Center** were completely deleted. Additionally, his professional LinkedIn account **Dr. Sabri Samirah** and Twitter account **@sbribrahim** vanished altogether. Even the Twitter account for Samirah's UMMA organization **@ourumma** was scrubbed of activity with only three tweets left now; the Twitter account has dropped accounts it is following and has a reduced number of followers. And finally, the Project M/Project Mobilize website no longer exists.

RISE OF A BROTHERHOOD ORGANIZER: DEPORTATION, EXILE, AND RETURN

This chapter continues the Center's focus on the expanding role of the USCMO (United States Council of Muslim Organizations), the first political party in the U.S. to be openly affiliated with the jihadist Muslim Brotherhood. The emergence in 2014 of Sabri Samirah, a Jordanian banned from entry to the U.S. since 2003, but allowed back in eleven years later, as a key leadership figure and political organizer within the USCMO, marks an important stage in the Brotherhood's "settlement process" as it seeks to expand its influence in American politics. The story of his rise through the ranks of the Muslim Brotherhood and into the U.S. political scene follows.

SAMIRAH'S LEADERSHIP WITH MUSLIM BROTHERHOOD IN U.S. BEFORE 2003 DEPORTATION

Prior to his 2003 deportation from the United States, Samirah served as President of the United Muslim Americans Association (UMAA) from 1999 to 2003. Interestingly, and illustrative of the overlapping leadership typical of the Brotherhood's U.S. network of organizations, the UMAA just happened to share office space with the Islamic Association for Palestine (IAP) in Palos Hills, Illinois. In a letter[154] dated 1 November 2000, Samirah, President of the UMAA, wrote to Rafeeq Jaber, President of the Islamic Association for Palestine and Secretary General of the UMAA Board of Trustees, to tell him that "The IAP, and all of its workers, and supporters are carrying a mission of central importance in the faith, civilization, history, and future of Muslims, Arabs, and Palestinians in America and around the globe." In addition to his UMAA presidency, Samirah simultaneously also had worked with Jaber and was Chairman of the IAP.

In Samirah's capacity as a Muslim Brotherhood leader working for IAP and UMAA in the United States, it is essential to understand the connections between IAP and HAMAS and the Muslim Brotherhood

---

[154] The Investigative Project on Terrorism, Islamic Association for Palestine 4th Annual Convention: "All Palestine Is Sacred," 23-25 November 2000. http://www.investigativeproject.org/documents/misc/438.pdf

nexuses for individuals who still hold positions of leadership today in the U.S.

In 1981, HAMAS operative Mousa Abu Marzook[155] established the Islamic Association for Palestine[156], in part to create for HAMAS a U.S. organization that would be able to deny any links to HAMAS. On 8 October 1987, the United States Department of State (US DoS) designated HAMAS as a Foreign Terrorist Organization (FTO). The IAP later would be parent to the Council on American Islamic Relations[157] (CAIR), which was incorporated in 1994 by IAP leadership Nihad Awad[158], Omar Ahmad[159], and Rafeeq Jaber.[160]

LEGAL CRITERIA FOR DESIGNATION OF A FOREIGN TERRORIST ORGANIZATION

Per the United States Department of State,[161] Foreign Terrorist Organizations are "designated by the Secretary of State in accordance with section 219 of the Immigration and Nationality Act (INA). FTO designations play a critical role in the fight against terrorism and are an effective means of curtailing support for terrorist activities."

Under Section 219 of the INA as amended, the Legal Criteria for Designation of a FTO[162] are as follows:

1. It must be a foreign organization.

---

[155] Steven Emerson, The Investigative Project on Terrorism, "Individual Terrorists: Mousa Abu Marzook," 20 April 2012.
http://www.investigativeproject.org/profile/106

[156] Steven Emerson, The Investigative Project on Terrorism, Government Exhibit 003-0003 3:04-CR-240-G U.S. v. HLF, et al, Bate # ISE-SW IB23/0002005,
http://www.investigativeproject.org/documents/case_docs/439.pdf

[157] Steven Emerson, The Investigative Project on Terrorism, "Groups and Networks: The Council on American-Islamic Relations (CAIR)," 15 July 2008.
http://www.investigativeproject.org/profile/172

[158] Steven Emerson, The Investigative Project on Terrorism, "Apologists or Extremists: Nihad Awad," 4 August 2010.
http://www.investigativeproject.org/profile/113

[159] Steven Emerson, The Investigative Project on Terrorism, IPT News, "The Case Against Omar Ahmad," 25 April 2011.
http://www.investigativeproject.org/2790/the-case-against-omar-ahmad

[160] Steven Emerson, The Investigative Project on Terrorism, "Apologists or Extremists: Rafeeq Jaber," 9 July 2008.
http://www.investigativeproject.org/profile/117

[161] U.S. Department of State, Chapter 6. Foreign Terrorist Organizations, Bureau of Counterterrorism: Country Reports on Terrorism 2013,
http://www.state.gov/j/ct/rls/crt/2013/224829.htm

[162] Ibid

2. The organization must engage in terrorist activity, as defined in section 212 (a)(3)(B) of the INA (8 U.S.C. § 1182(a)(3)(B)), or terrorism, as defined in section 140(d)(2) of the Foreign Relations Authorization Act, Fiscal Years 1988 and 1989 (22 U.S.C. § 2656f(d)(2)), or retain the capability and intent to engage in terrorist activity or terrorism.

3. The organization's terrorist activity or terrorism must threaten the security of U.S. nationals or the national security (national defense, foreign relations, or the economic interests) of the United States.

As shown by court documents[163], the IAP was a prong of the Muslim Brotherhood's Palestine Committee[164], until the U.S. government froze IAP's assets and shut it down in December 2004 on grounds that it was funding terrorism. The IAP was named as one of the Muslim Brotherhood's twenty-nine likeminded "organizations of our friends" in the May 1991 Muslim Brotherhood[165] document "An Explanatory Memorandum on the General Strategic Goal for the Group in North America."

SAMIRAH'S MOBILIZATION OF THE UNITED MUSLIM AMERICANS ASSOCIATION

Samirah, who had praised Jaber's work with the IAP, stated that his UMAA organization was "working on politically empowering our Muslim and Arab American community; a front that we believe – in one of its manifestations – will help advancing justice for Palestine and the Palestinian people[166]." His political abilities were not to be confined only to the Muslim community, but took direct and calculated aim at established U.S. political figures and parties, including the Governor and Illinois General Assembly, including both Democratic and Republican leadership. The screenshot of the

---

[163] Steven Emerson, The Investigative Project on Terrorism, Government Exhibit 003-0003 3:04-CR-240-G U.S. v. HLF, et al, Bate #HE-SW 1B72/0000801, http://www.investigativeproject.org/documents/case_docs/438.pdf

[164] Steven Emerson, The Investigative Project on Terrorism, "Bylaws of the Palestine Committee of the Muslim Brotherhood by Palestine Committee," Date Unknown, http://www.investigativeproject.org/document/id/24

[165] Discover the Networks, "Muslim Brotherhood," http://www.discoverthenetworks.org/groupProfile.asp?grpid=6386

[166] Steven Emerson, The Investigative Project on Terrorism, The Investigative Project on Terrorism, Islamic Association for Palestine 4th Annual Convention: "All Palestine Is Sacred," 23-25 November 2000 http://www.investigativeproject.org/documents/misc/438.pdf

following photo collage is from Samirah's Facebook page. He describes the photos as the following:

> Pics from a Candidates Night 2002, and a pic when signing the Halal Food Act by former Governor of IL. **George Ryan.** Pics include now Governor Pat Quinn[167], IL Senate GOP Christine Radogno[168], back then Chairman of the CIOGC **Kareem Irfan, Dr. Jamal Badawi, Shaikh Jamal Said, Dr. Abdel Elsiddig,** and **Sammer Ghouleh.** All of a younger age I will search for more pics of others and the community, and post them for "Memory of Public Life". — with Abdel Elsiddig[169] and Sammer Ghouleh[170].

Sabri Samirah and Candidates Night 2002 and Halal Food Act Signing with Governor George Ryan

Before his ban from the United States, Samirah mobilized the UMAA and 450,000 Muslims in Illinois in the successful bipartisan passage of the Halal Food Act, Senate Bill 750.[171] On his Facebook page for the American and Middle-Eastern Affairs Center Think Tank, Samirah states he was "the first Muslim[172] to make a testimony on behalf of the Muslim community and a Muslim issue at the State Senate." In the following

---

[167] Pat Quinn Politician Facebook page, https://www.facebook.com/GovernorQuinn
[168] Christine Radogno Government Official Facebook page, https://www.facebook.com/cradogno
[169] Abdel Elsiddig Facebook page, https://www.facebook.com/abdel.elsiddig
[170] Sammer Ghouleh Facebook page, https://www.facebook.com/sammer.ghouleh
[171] Illinois Government News Network: Governor's Office Press Release, "Governor Ryan Signs "Halal Food Act"," 16 August 2001. http://www3.illinois.gov/PressReleases/ShowPressRelease.cfm?SubjectID=3&RecNum=1517
[172] Sabri Samirah Facebook page for American and Middle-Eastern Affairs Center Think Tank, "About," https://www.facebook.com/AMEACThinkTank/info, accessed 15 November 2014

screenshot of a statement[173] from Albawaba News on 20 August 2001, Samirah's integral leadership role on the Halal Food Act is mentioned. As shown in the following screenshot of the 92nd General Assembly Status of SB0750[174], one of the bill's nine sponsors in the Illinois General Assembly was then-State Senator Barack Obama, a Democrat from Chicago. Obama was added as Chief Cosponsor on 20 March 2001.

```
         FISCAL NOTE (Department of Agriculture)
         SB 750 would not impose any additional cost on the Department
         to implement. The Department could comply with the increased
         number of inspections with its current existing staff and
         resources.
FEB-21-2001  S  FIRST READING
FEB-21-2001  S  REFERRED TO SENATE RULES COMMITTEE         RULES
FEB-28-2001  S     ASSIGNED TO COMMITTEE                   PUBLIC HEALTH
MAR-20-2001  S                            POSTPONED
MAR-20-2001  S  ADDED AS A CHIEF CO-SPONSOR                WALSH,L
MAR-20-2001  S  ADDED AS A CO-SPONSOR                      SMITH
MAR-20-2001  S  ADDED AS A CHIEF CO-SPONSOR                OBAMA
MAR-21-2001  S  ADDED AS A CHIEF CO-SPONSOR                VIVERITO
MAR-21-2001  S  ADDED AS A CO-SPONSOR                      HENDON
MAR-22-2001  S  ADDED AS A CHIEF CO-SPONSOR                SILVERSTEIN
```

Halal Food Act, Senate Bill 750 Status, Illinois 92nd General Assembly

On 16 August 2001, less than one month before the fateful events of 11 September 2001, the bill was signed into law by Illinois Republican Governor George Ryan.

Halal Food Act press release from Office of Illinois Governor George Ryan

On 22 January 2004, after Samirah's unsuccessful efforts to return to this country following his deportation executed by U.S. Attorney General

[173] Mohammed Ayub Khan, "US Muslims Praise Bill on 'Halal Food'," Albawaba News, 20 August 2001. http://www.albawaba.com/news/us-muslims-praise-bill-%E2%80%98halal-food%E2%80%99

[174] Illinois General Assembly, 92nd General Assembly, Status of SB0750, http://www.ilga.gov/legislation/legisnet92/status/920SB0750.html

John Ashcroft, the United Muslim Americans Association (UMAA) was dissolved, according to the website of the Illinois secretary of state, as shown in the following screenshot.

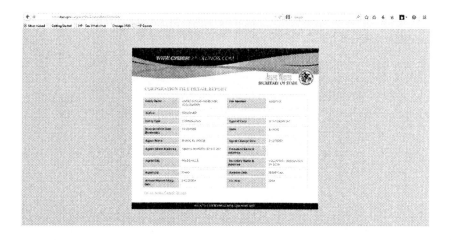

Dissolution of United Muslim Americans Association (UMAA)

SAMIRAH LAUNCHES THE MUSLIM BROTHERHOOD "UNIFIED VOTING BLOCK" 2014 CAMPAIGN

In the absence of Samirah's leadership due to his deportation, the UMAA website[175] also became defunct. After a decade passed, however, Samirah would call for a gathering of Muslim Brotherhood leadership in August 2014. Samirah planned to host the event[176] at the building of the Muslim American Society[177] (MAS), an overt arm[178] of the Muslim Brotherhood in America, next door to the Mosque Foundation in Bridgeview, Illinois on Tuesday, 5 August 2014.

---

[175] Former UMAA Website: http://www.theumaa.org/
[176] Sabri Samirah Facebook page for American and Middle-Eastern Affairs Center Think Tank, https://www.facebook.com/events/1460809087502948/permalink/14634224172416 15/, accessed 15 November 2014
[177] Steven Emerson, The Investigative Project on Terrorism, "Muslim American Society: The Investigative Project on Terrorism Dossier," 10 September 2007. http://www.investigativeproject.org/documents/misc/44.pdf
[178] Steven Emerson, The Investigative Project on Terrorism, United States Court of Appeals for the Fourth Circuit, No. 07-4778, *United States of America, Plaintiff-Appellee v. Sabri Benkahla Defendant-Appellant* http://www.investigativeproject.org/documents/case_docs/542.pdf#page=58

🔊 Public · Meetup · Hosted by American and Middle-Eastern Affairs Center ...

🕐 Tuesday at 6:30pm - 9:30pm
Next Week

📍 MAS Building, 9210 S Oketo Ave Bridgeview, IL 60457

Now, Important, Confirm Attendance
On Tuesday, Aug. 5th, 2014, 6:30-9:30 PM
At MAS Building, Next to Mosque Foundation, Bridgeview, IL.

Invite Others & "Share" this Historical Meeting

Effectively, Support your Community & Issues, Including Gaza, through
Sustained Public & Political Empowerment. It is Shame on us that Our
Government Supports Israeli Occupation and Terrorism. ACT, NOW.
Confirm Attendance.

Why to attend: to develop & empower our community in public and political
life, in order for us to, appropriately & effectively, protect & serve our
interests & issues -locally, nationally & internationally, i.e. Palestine.

Who should attend: community leaders, influencers, activists, experts of
public fields (governmental, media, political, economic, social, educational,
youth, women, legal, health, immigrants...), and volunteers from all diverse
backgrounds and domains of Muslim & Arab community, including women
& young leaders.

The meeting agenda will address the suggestion to establish a new
community grassroots organization to be called "United Muslim & Arab
Americans Association" (UMAAA), and to propose a follow up committee,
an interim Board of Trustees, an Advisory Council, and/or interim
Executive Committee.
#SupportGaza #AJAGAZA

POSTS

"Unified Voting Block" 2014 Campaign

At this point, after only being in the U.S. for less than six months, Samirah was now both the President of the newly established American and Middle Eastern Affairs Center Think Tank[179] (AMEAC) and CEO of the Development Institute for Consultation & Training, LLC, (DICT).[180] Below is a screenshot from the Illinois Secretary of State's office with the

---

[179] Sabri Samirah Facebook page for American and Middle-Eastern Affairs Center Think Tank https://www.facebook.com/AMEACThinkTank, accessed 15 November 2014

[180] Sabri Samirah LinkedIn Profile, http://www.linkedin.com/in/sabrisamirah

corporation file detail report for AMEAC with an incorporation date of 04/04/2014.

Illinois Incorporation Report for the American and Middle Eastern Affairs Center Think Tank

So, it's clear that even by that point, he was already well-positioned to launch the next steps intended to advance the introduction of Muslim Brotherhood entities into the U.S. political system.

Samirah stated[181] on the Facebook event page that the August 2014 "historic" meeting agenda "will address the suggestion to establish a new community grassroots organization to be called 'United Muslim & Arab Americans Association' (UMAAA)." Due to space limitations, however, the meeting was eventually held at the Universal School.

The following screenshot advertised this upcoming meeting scheduled for 5 August 2014 and is a good illustration of the Brotherhood's political agenda, given its messages to "Help Strengthen Our Political Power" and "Register & Vote."

---

[181] Sabri Samirah Facebook page, https://www.facebook.com/events/1460809087502948/?source=1, accessed 15 November 2014

Sabri Samirah's AMEAC "Unified Voting Bloc" August 2014 Facebook advertisement

Samirah's earlier success thirteen years ago in 2001 with the creation of a "Unified Block of Voters" provided him a good working model as he reinitiated this "Unified Voting Block" for the 2014 midterm election cycle. In his letter[182] posted on a Facebook event page from 31 July 2014, Samirah reminded his audience, "Let us not forget the critical role our American policy plays in, blindly, supporting the Israeli occupation and the atrocities they commit with our American tax-money, arms, diplomacy, veto, and alliances around the globe. It is our direct responsibility to change all of that, effectively and strategically; through the building of a solid influence over elected officials, elections and policy-making."

The following screenshot from his Facebook page for AMEAC shows questions provided in advance to prepare those from the community who would attend this meeting.

---

[182] Sabri Samirah Facebook page, https://www.facebook.com/events/1460809087502948/permalink/14634224172416 15/, accessed 15 November 2014

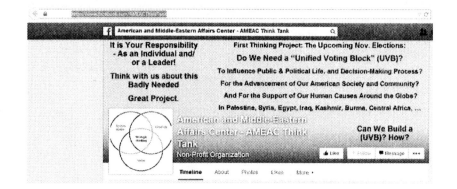

AMEAC: "Do We Need a "Unified Voting Block" (UVB)?"

On Tuesday, 5 August 2014, just over 70 individuals (including more than one dozen women and even one school age child) from the Muslim and Arab communities were in attendance for a presentation given by Samirah. The following screenshots are from the Facebook page for Samirah's think tank AMEAC.

Sabri Samirah's AMEAC presentation at Universal School

Audience gathered at Universal School to hear Sabri
Samirah's community mobilization plans

Those individuals who gathered for a 2 ½ hour program at the Universal School that evening comprised primarily activists and community leaders from the Chicago metropolitan area and Milwaukee, Wisconsin. Distinguished political guests included Moon Khan (former Republican York Township Trustee turned Democrat, and President, Asian-American Caucus of Dupage County, who was also a past chairman for the Islamic Society of North America's National Convention's Media Relations Committee) and Nasir Jahangir (2nd vice Chair, Democrat Party of Dupage County).

The initial meeting was an airing of issues considered important to the Muslim community with suggestions for how to solve perceived obstacles that prevented their community from gaining full political empowerment in U.S. society. There was additional talk of stopping Congress from funding Israel, and that Islam/Shariah should be rightfully recognized as a legitimate religion in all of the U.S. The general direction of the discussion as led by Samirah focused on mastery of the operational mechanics of the political process in the U.S. and how to advance Muslim political objectives.

Samirah took advice from individuals about who should be appointed as activists, advisors, community leaders, and subject matter experts to help him with AMEAC's work in the Muslim community and the development of his UMAA group. At the conclusion of the event led by Samirah, a follow up meeting was set to determine what could be accomplished with a more specific action plan. The stage was set for the lead-up to the November 2014 election.

UMAA RISING: USCMO TAKES AIM AT ILLINOIS POLITICS

In this chapter about the United States Council of Muslim Organizations, the first U.S. political party openly associated with the jihadist Muslim Brotherhood, the rise of the UMMA (not an acronym but the full name of the group) follows shortly after the return of Sabri Samirah, member of the Jordanian Muslim Brotherhood, to the U.S. following eleven years of exile. Once Samirah's travel ban was lifted by the Obama administration in early 2014, he returned quickly to the U.S. and launched into a busy schedule of appearances and speeches to galvanize the U.S. Muslim community to political activism.

MUSLIM BROTHERHOOD LAUNCHES "GET OUT THE VOTE" CAMPAIGN INITIATIVE

By 23 September 2014, Samirah's new organization, UMMA, which succeeded UMAA (United Muslim Americans Association) to promote the political ambitions of the Muslim Brotherhood formally, had been established with the Illinois Secretary of State's office. The following picture is a screenshot from the Illinois Secretary of State's office with the corporation file detail report for UMMA where Sabri Samirah is named as the registered agent.

Illinois Incorporation Report for UMMA

While Samirah had publicly announced the news through Twitter and Facebook that the new community grassroots organization was to be tentatively named the United Muslim & Arab Americans Association (UMAAA), the official announcement dated 3 October 2014 declared the name as UMMA, which was to be associated with a forthcoming website at www.OurUMMA.org.

Per one of his Facebook pages[183] Samirah describes UMMA as "a registered, not-for-profit, nonpartisan, and grassroots organization, dedicated to promoting the public and political empowerment of the American Muslim community and serve its interests." Additionally, a preview for UMMA's first event scheduled for 14 October 2014 appears in the following screenshots from Samirah's Twitter and Facebook accounts.

---

[183] UMMA Facebook page, "Page Info," https://www.facebook.com/pages/UMMA/372928419538735?sk=info&tab=page_info, accessed 15 November 2014

Tweets about UMMA's first event from Sabri Samirah's Twitter account

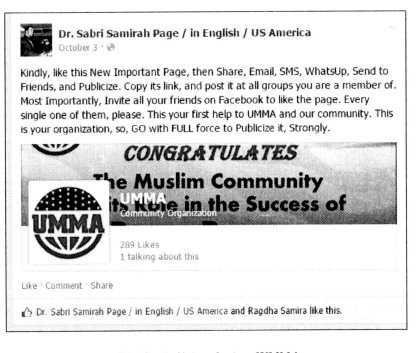

Sabri Samirah's introduction of UMMA

American and Middle-Eastern Affairs Center - AMEAC Think Tank
shared UMMA's photo
October 3

Please, attend and invite your friends.

Share, Email, SMS, WhatsUp, Send to Friends, and Publicize

Like · Comment · Share

Facebook advertisement for UMMA's first event

When the UMMA held its first candidates' forum on 14 October 2014 in Dupage County, several dozen candidates spoke to the audience numbering around 100 individuals. The vast majority of the local, state, and federal candidates were Democrats with the exception of a handful of Republicans. As noted on the UMMA website, "The goal is to communicate with and educate candidates and officials, and ask them to respond. Let us have no illusion, the stronger constituency we are, the more forthcoming they will be toward us. We should have no wishful thinking! Yet, we have great numbers and resources. Once we have a stronger role in elections, everybody will be seeking our support!"[184] It was made clear at this initial candidates' forum that if the Muslim community delivered votes translating to key victories for candidates, then future candidate forums could involve 100 or more candidates seeking Muslim votes.

In a post to the Muslim community from his Facebook page, Samirah made the following points[185] on 17 October 2014 regarding the promotion of candidates:

> In addition, UMMA's endorsements, fully take into consideration political realities, electoral competitions, future strategic calculations, our community's concentrations, and common interests with other communities. Officials, candidates, political parties, and the media will take us more seriously in the future because of our effective and unified actions of today.
> In finalizing this list, UMMA's bottom line measure is to make sure that candidates effectively and publicly RECOGNIZE rights and interests of our community. Gradually, our community should be accepted as an integral part of the larger society and a player in the public decision-making process.
> Indeed, NO ONE will listen to our grievances if we are not a strong player in the game and/or are only shouting from the sidelines! Before we ask with high expectations and/or hopelessness, we need to show our strong participation and unified leadership. Many other society's segments have done it.

These points from Samirah's post confirm what was previously discussed at the meetings held on 5 August 2014 in Bridgeview, Illinois and 14 October 2014 in Willowbrook, Illinois. Appearing on the UMMA website, the following page "Issues and Positions of the Muslim

---

[184] UMMA Website, http://ourumma.org, accessed 1 November 2014
[185] Dr. Sabri Samirah Facebook page,
https://www.facebook.com/DrSabriSamirahPageInEnglishUsAmerica, accessed 24 October 2014

Community, UMMA Serves[186]" is a delineation of fourteen specified areas of importance for the UMMA to present to candidates and officials.

According to a rather exaggerated estimate at the UMMA website, there are about 7 million Muslims in the U.S. (The actual number is likely closer to about 3 million.) Per their figures for the State of Illinois from the UMMA, there an estimated 500,000 Muslims with 400,000 of those in the greater Chicago area (250,000 in Cook County and 150,000 in Du Page and surrounding counties). The UMMA also notes that Muslims may account for up to 15% of the population in some congressional and state districts, and cities and villages in northeastern Illinois. While these numbers probably are at least somewhat exaggerated, UMMA's intent and objectives are clear: encourage political involvement of that segment of the electorate that self-identifies as "Muslim" to create a voting bloc that candidates and parties will seek out for support in future elections.

STAR SPANGLED SHARIAH AND THE MUSLIM BROTHERHOOD

When the UMMA website was launched in October 2014, a series of photos appeared in the banner section. The screenshots of the following pictures offer an example of what appears on Samirah's UMMA website, obviously seeking to portray a patriotic message from the Muslim Brotherhood. This includes a picture of Islamic minarets superimposed on the American flag. A picture of President Barack Obama stating "The future must not belong to those who slander the prophet of Islam" mysteriously disappeared from the website.

---

[186]UMMA Website, http://www.ourumma.org/issues.html, accessed 1 November 2014

Issues And Positions Of The Muslim Community, UMMA Serves

Muslim Brotherhood Co-opts non-Muslim Communities to Influence Elections

Samirah's research to determine Muslim population centers in jurisdictions where they can affect key election outcomes is indicative of his underlying strategy for the Muslim Brotherhood to establish a unified voting bloc. Launching an ambitious voter mobilization program aligned with key issues sets the stage for future elections. This strategy emerged clearly at the August 2014 meetings when Samirah and those present discussed co-opting non-Muslim (especially African American) communities with which Muslims propose to join in solidarity on such themes as civil rights issues, in return for these communities backing issues of prime importance to the Muslim community.

Before USCMO member Islamic Center of Wheaton hosted Samirah and the UMMA on 18 October 2014, Samirah sent a message with a sense of urgency regarding the Muslim community participating in the midterm election. This was for strategic purposes as the UMMA political endorsements of candidates favorable to the Muslim community were promised several weeks before the November 2014 midterm election. The following is a screenshot from the UMMA's Facebook page with a notice from Samirah.

UMMA
October 17 · Edited

!!Urgent !!!عاجل

Dear Community Leaders & Activists
Please, DO NOT be ABSENT!!! Unless it is a life or death experience, God
(Forbids (Read more below

يا قيادات ونشطاء الجالية المسلمة والعربية في شيكاغو
ا "ولا يأب الشهداء إذا ما دعوا"، "وفقوهم إنهم مسؤولون"، "إن الله لا يغير..."، "وقل
إعملوا.."، أنتم قيادات وهذه نعرتكم، لا تبكوا وتصرخوا في الحطب والشوارع على
أحوالنا والحل بأيديكم يبدأ مع "الأمة".. "اللهم إني قد بلغت اللهم فإشهد".. "والله
حسيبكم".. وسيسألكم عن "رعيتكم".. ولا مجال لكم للتهرب من المسؤولية فهي
في أحضانكم وهنا في بلدكم أمريكا.. ولا تلقوها على الظالمين في عالمنا
الإسلامي.. ولا تحذلوا أنفسكم وجاليتكم وأمنكم وقضاياكم والمظلومين في كل
مكان ".. لا يسلمه ولا يخذله ولا يظلمه"..!!! ... "وستذكرون ما أقول لكم".. "بل
الإنسان على نفسه بصيرة ولو ألقى معاذيره".. "وكل يأتيه يوم القيامة فردا".. والله
إن ما أقوله لكم هو الحق كما أنكم تنطقون.. فلا تهربوا من مسؤولياتكم!!!!!!! ا

والله لا نكلمكم أكثر من طاقتكم. وهي إجتماعات قليلة جدا!! فلم الخذلان!!؟؟؟ا

++++++++++++++++++++++
For Immediate Release & Community High Publicity

UMMA Invites You to HELP CHOOSE Candidates for Endorsement to Our
Community

UMMA's "Endorsement List" for 2014 General Elections, the ONLY of its Kind,
will be Highly Publicized via Our Half Million Community Networks, Outlets,
& Centers, UMMA's Mass Mailing, E-Mailing, Social Media
www.OurUMMA.org

:Come to UMMA's Meeting
Saturday, Oct. 18th, 2014, at 11:00 AM
Islamic Center of Wheaton
E. Geneva Rd, Wheaton, IL 60187 900

Urgent Message from Sabri Samirah about UMMA event at USCMO member
Islamic Center of Wheaton

MUSLIM BROTHERHOOD ENDORSES GUBERNATORIAL REPUBLICAN CANDIDATE BRUCE RAUNER

Five days after Samirah's UMMA made its presentation at USCMO member Islamic Center of Wheaton, the UMMA announced on Facebook on 23 October 2014 that its endorsed candidates list was close to publication. The breaking news from the UMMA, however, came when Samirah announced on 26 October 2014 its endorsement of Illinois Republican gubernatorial candidate Bruce Rauner. The following screenshots from the UMMA's Facebook page and website provide details that stunned even the Muslim community, which had strongly supported outgoing Democratic Governor Pat Quinn.

Muslim Brotherhood endorsement of Illinois Gubernatorial Candidate Republican Bruce Rauner

UMMA
October 26 · Edited

Kindly, Highly, PUBLICIZE.... NOW !!!
STAY TUNED... MORE to COME!!!
Share, send to your email lists, text, whats-up and post at all of your groups, organizations and friends' pages and email lists.
Kindly, send us any of your questions and/or comments in a private message and/or as a public post. All opinions are welcome, yet, NO hostile language will be allowed. You my comment objectively, respectfully, and with specific facts as they pertain to the Muslim community common interests, and, specifically, on the race of the Governor of IL as a local and specific endorsement.
UMMA will soon publish a full report of why this endorsement after its very extensive process of selection and consultation with all parts of the Muslim community.
It is important to note that UMMA is acting in a non-partisan way, and most of its other Federal, State, and county endorsements were of democratic candidates. UMMA endorses on a case by case basis.
Stay Tuned... MORE to COME!!!

 BREAKING NEWS
UMMA
-Political Leader of Muslims-
Endorses Republican

Bruce Rauner
& Evelyn Sanguinetti
for IL Governor & Lt. Governor, 2014

Like · Comment · Share   👍3 💬3 ↗ 35 Shares

UMMA breaking news BruceRauner endorsement on Facebook

Muslim Brotherhood Letter Explanation for Rauner Endorsement

In a letter, which no longer appears on the UMMA website, to Muslims after the announcement of the UMMA endorsement for Rauner, key points made for the decision included the following:

> With its highly publicized endorsements of 85% of Democratic candidates, 15% of Republican hopefuls for general elections, and [R]epublican Bruce Rauner for Illinois' Governor, it seems UMMA has been successful in achieving parts of its vision and strategy.
> Our community, leaders, and organizations, became engaged in an attempt to play an active role in the upcoming elections. Parties, candidates and leaders are paying attention to our community's role and influence, and try to more effectively reach out to us! UMMA wanted to be a catalyst for the change, and it seems it has achieved this!
> UMMA has shared at length at its leadership meetings before it made its endorsement, all details about its meeting and communications with Rauner, Sanguinetti, and his campaign, including the methods for evaluation that were implemented in the decision making process. Based on very objective and sensitive criteria, UMMA leadership felt that Rauner has fulfilled the requirements for our endorsement.
> In short, Rauner has reached out to us, met UMMA leadership after two days of communications, found nothing objectionable in UMMA's list of issues and positions, would not affect whatever our community has with Quinn, would continue the open access to his office if elected, and desires to attend our community's gatherings. His Lt. Governor's candidate Evelyn Sanguinetti herself has visited the Islamic Foundation of Villa Park, and she has been in touch with the Muslim community.

On 4 November 2014, Rauner won his bid to be the next governor of Illinois. The following screenshots are of pictures posted by Samirah on his Facebook page and the UMMA website. They show him and members of the UMMA leadership with incoming Illinois Governor-elect Rauner.

*Sabri Samirah (third from right) standing directly to left of
Illinois Governor-Elect Bruce Rauner*

UMMA Celebration with Illinois Governor-Elect Bruce Rauner on 4 November 2014

Samirah's newly established UMMA demonstrates through its political activism that it functions as an operational arm of the U.S. Council of Muslim Organizations (USCMO), designed to help further USCMO goals and objectives. Three months prior to the midterm November 2014 elections, Samirah led a meeting on 5 August 2014 in Bridgeview, Illinois with Muslim Brotherhood leadership to discuss a new organization to mobilize the Muslim community to become actively engaged in the political process. His description then of the main goal for the group's agenda was "to be as much as inclusive, unifying, open, and fair in order for us to achieve the highest level of grassroots participation, unity, representation and legitimacy in serving, representing, and leading our community, publicly and politically." This is broadly congruent with the mission of the first U.S. Muslim Brotherhood political party. In the short time since Samirah has been back in the U.S., he has worked proactively with the leadership of USCMO member organizations, assisted with fundraising, appointed new leadership in the community, and mobilized Muslim voters. Looking ahead to the 2016 presidential campaign, it seems likely that the USCMO, UMMA, and Samirah will be at the forefront of efforts to energize the U.S. Muslim electorate on behalf of the Muslim Brotherhood.

As the 13th Annual Muslim American Society and Islamic Circle of North America Convention in Chicago was set to begin on Christmas Day 2014, Congressman André Carson was preparing to address Muslim Brotherhood leadership in Chicago. The timing could not have been more opportune, as USCMO member Islamic Circle of North America had just revealed[187] on 5 December 2014 the USCMO's plans to "host the first-of-its-kind National Muslim Advocacy Day on Capitol Hill in Washington, D.C." in the Spring of 2015. Congressman Carson seemed the ideal choice by the Muslim Brotherhood to rally the masses, given his long-standing, close relationship with so many Brotherhood affiliates – as well as the financial support many of them have provided to him over the years.

---

[187] Islamic Circle of North America, "Muslims to hold a united Capitol Hill Advocacy Day," 5 December 2014. http://www.icna.org/u-s-muslims-to-hold-first-united-capitol-hill-advocacy-day/, accessed 6 December 2014

U.S. MUSLIM BROTHERHOOD POLITICAL PARTY FINANCIALLY SUPPORTS CONGRESSMAN ANDRÉ CARSON

The Muslim American Society (MAS) and Islamic Circle of North America (ICNA) held their 13th annual convention at the McCormick Center in President Barack Obama's hometown of Chicago from 25-28 December 2014. Notable among the scheduled contributors at this gathering of high level international and national leadership representing the jihadist Muslim Brotherhood was keynote speaker U.S. Congressman André Carson, a Democrat from Indiana's 7th District. The presence at this convention of an elected U.S. lawmaker who has received financial donations from Muslim Brotherhood-affiliated organizations ever since he was first elected to the House of Representatives in a special election in early 2008 must be a matter of serious concern.

CONGRESSMAN CARSON'S ON-AGAIN, OFF-AGAIN MUSLIM BROTHERHOOD SPEAKING ENGAGEMENT

Controversy surrounds the appearance of Congressman Carson at the MAS-ICNA 2014 Convention in Chicago where he was a scheduled panelist together with Mazen Mokhtar, National Executive Director for the Muslim American Society, which was founded as the U.S. branch of the Muslim Brotherhood. Worse yet, according to the testimony[188] of federal agents in federal courts, MAS National Executive Director Mokhtar facilitated operations for running an Al-Qa'eda website responsible for raising funds[189] for the Taliban. In March 2014, MAS was just one of several Muslim Brotherhood-affiliates that joined together to establish the U.S. Council of Muslim Organizations (USCMO), the first U.S. political

---

[188] Dana Priest and Susan Schmidt, "Terror Suspect's Arrest Opens New Inquiries," *Washington Post*, 8 August 2004. http://www.washingtonpost.com/wp-dyn/articles/A48936-2004Aug7.html

[189] Patrick Poole "Muslim Congressman's Ferguson Panel at Chicago Islamic Convention Features Al-Qaeda Webmaster, Taliban Fundraiser," *PJ Media*, 27 December 2014. http://pjmedia.com/tatler/2014/12/27/muslim-congressmans-ferguson-panel-at-chicago-islamic-convention-features-al-qaeda-webmaster-taliban-fundraiser/

party openly founded by members of the North American Brotherhood network.

At the December 2014 MAS-ICNA Convention, Carson and Mokhtar were scheduled to speak on a panel addressing "Ferguson Is Our Issue: We Can't Breathe." The following picture is from the actual program of the MAS-ICNA 2014 Convention issued to attendees, which clearly shows that Congressman Carson was scheduled to appear on a panel 26 December 2014 with Mazen Mokhtar, the executive director of USCMO member MAS National. (The program date is printed erroneously, as the last Saturday in December 2014 was the 27th, not the 26th). Nevertheless, Carson's later official statement that he didn't even find out about this panel until sometime on Sunday 28 December seems questionable.

*13th Annual MAS-ICNA 2014 Convention featuring
Congressman Carson and Mazen Mokhtar*

Prior to his scheduled appearance on this panel for Saturday evening, Congressman Carson did make an appearance as scheduled as the keynote speaker for the 13th Annual MAS-ICNA Convention Appreciation Dinner—after which he seems to have disappeared, with no comment from the Convention organizers about the empty seat at the Ferguson panel. The following picture is a screenshot from the MAS-ICNA 2014 convention website providing details for his appearance.

Meet the Celebrity!

13th Annual MAS-ICNA Convention Appreciation Dinner

Grab your chance for a one-on-one encounter with your favorite speakers and performers.
This is a great opportunity for you to have a close up with people who make this convention possible!

JOIN US FOR THIS ELEGANT DINNER AND ONE OF KIND EXPERIENCE!

Keynote Speaker

Congressman Andre' Carson

Representative for Indiana's 7th Congressional District

Quran Recitation & Dua'a

Shiekh Mohammad Jebril

When

Saturday, December twenty-seven
two thousand fourteen
at five o'clock in the evening

At

McCormick Place Convention Center
Vista Room (Room # S406)
2301 S. Lake Shore Drive. Chicago, IL 60616

13th Annual MAS-ICNA Convention Appreciation Dinner with Congressman Carson

There is no question the Congressman was present at the Convention Center on the date in question. The following images are from Muslim Brotherhood leader Sabri Samirah's organization UMMA and UMMA Board of Trustee member and chairman Darwish Mabruk's Facebook pages, showing photos taken during the MAS-ICNA convention where Congressman Carson is pictured meeting with various Muslim Brotherhood leadership figures, apparently just prior to the dinner.

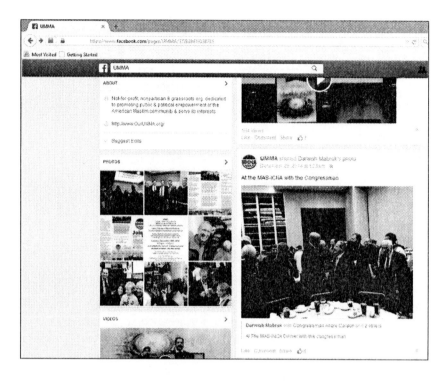

UMMA promoting Congressman Carson with Muslim Brotherhood at
13ᵗʰ Annual MAS-ICNA Convention

UMMA Chairman Darwish Mabruk with Congressman Carson

CONGRESSMAN CARSON BACKPEDALS ABOUT ATTENDANCE AT CHICAGO MAS-ICNA CONVENTION

Later, as the back-pedaling began, Congressman Carson issued a press statement on 31 December 2014 as shown in the screenshot below from his official Twitter account. In both the press statement and Tweet, however, he strangely neglected to mention the Muslim American Society, which was the co-sponsor of the MAS-ICNA Convention chaired by Hussein Ata (president, Mosque Foundation in Bridgeview, Illinois, where USCMO Secretary General Oussama Jammal is a past president and current Chairman of MAS-PACE).

Congressman Carson's Twitter account announcement about 13th Annual MAS-ICNA Convention

In Carson's statement that appears on his Congressional website[190], the following message was delivered to his constituency on 31 December 2014:

> **INDIANAPOLIS** -- Today, Congressman André Carson released the following statement in response to his attendance at the ICNA

---

[190]Congressman André Carson for the 7th District of Indiana, "Carson Statement on Attending the ICNA Chicago Convention," 31 December 2014. http://carson.house.gov/media-center/press-releases/carson-statement-on-his-attendance-at-the-icna-chicago-convention

(Islamic Circle of North America) Chicago convention last weekend.

On Saturday, December 27, I attended the ICNA Chicago convention to deliver a speech on the importance of civil engagement and developing leaders in the community.

On Sunday, December 28, I learned that ICNA had also scheduled me to sit on a Ferguson panel Saturday night – which I had not planned on participating in. At no point had I ever confirmed to attend any other events other than the dinner. Any reference to my participation or appearance on the Ferguson panel during the ICNA conference is not factual.

As a former law enforcement officer with the Indiana Department of Homeland Security in the anti-terrorism unit, it is critical that Americans know that I would never associate with any individual or organization trying to harm the United States of America or its citizens.

The absence of the Muslim American Society's name in Congressman Carson's press statement and Tweet is peculiar. It's not as though he'd avoided associating with MAS in the past—but of course, that was before the United Arab Emirates (UAE) listed MAS as a terrorist organization, as noted Patrick Poole.[191] But it's also not the first time Carson has attempted to conceal details of such problematic associations.

In June 2014, Congressman Carson was featured as a keynote speaker for the USCMO's inaugural banquet, an event shrouded in secrecy with no transcripts, audio, or video having been released, as would usually be customary. Both Congressman Carson and Congressman Keith Ellison (Democrat, MN-5th District) were invited by USCMO Secretary General Oussama Jammal to speak at the U.S. Muslim Brotherhood political party's event on 10 June 2014 at the Hilton Crystal City Hotel near Washington, D.C. To date, their respective congressional offices have refused to make publicly available either the text or video of the remarks delivered by Carson and Ellison at this high level Muslim Brotherhood function, held at a time when the Obama administration's foreign policy supporting Brotherhood revolutions in Egypt, Libya, and Syria was collapsing in failure.

So, perhaps the Congressmen's reticence might have something to do with the all-star Muslim Brotherhood line-up that attended that banquet, a couple of which groups, as noted above, were named in November 2014 by the UAE to its new terrorist organizations list (on that list are both CAIR

---

[191] Patrick Poole, "Congressman Walks Back Appearance at Islamic Terror Group's Chicago Convention," *PJ Media*, 1 January 2015.
http://pjmedia.com/tatler/2015/01/01/congressman-walks-back-appearance-at-islamic-terror-groups-chicago-convention/?print=1

and MAS, along with the Muslim Brotherhood itself.). As reported by the Muslim Link Paper for this historic Muslim Brotherhood leadership gathering, others in the speaker line-up included Dr. Ousama Jammal, Secretary General, USCMO; Dr. Osama Abu-Irshaid, Board Member, American Muslims for Palestine; Nihad Awad, National Executive Director, Council on American Islamic Relations (CAIR); Naeem Baig, President, Islamic Circle of North America (ICNA); Mazen Mokhtar, Executive Director, Muslim American Society (MAS); Khalil Meek, Executive Director, Muslim Legal Fund of America; Imam Delawar Hussein, Dr Lynne Muhammad, Founder, Making A Difference Through Discoveries, American Islamic College, Whitney Young Magnet High School; and W.D. Mohammed II, President, Mosque Cares.

Congressmen Carson and Ellison with USCMO leadership at
June 2014 Inaugural Banquet

Nor was the December 2014 MAS-ICNA Convention Carson's first appearance at the annual event. Two years prior to the June 2014 USCMO event launching the first ever U.S. Muslim Brotherhood political party, Congressman Carson participated at the MAS-ICNA summer 2012 convention. Striking a somewhat exaggerated tone of aggrieved victimhood, he told the gathering that "America must understand that she needs Muslims. There are over 7 million Muslims in this country. While we are under attack, we cannot retreat. We have been a part of America since the inception of America..." Congressman Carson continued, "Now, it is unfortunate that there are those who are thinking at this convention right now, we are having secret meetings that we are plotting to destroy this country. But I say to those who are here undercover, Allah will not allow you to stop us."

CONGRESSMAN CARSON'S NON-STELLAR SCORECARD ON NATIONAL SECURITY ISSUES

Despite his attempt at projecting a patriotic image, though, Congressman Carson's congressional voting record on national security issues demonstrates a rather different profile. On 15 October 2014, the Center for Security Policy released its 11ᵗʰ annual 2013-2014 **Congressional National Security Scorecard for the 113th Congress.**[192] The Center scored a total of 27 votes in the U.S. House of Representatives, and 15 votes in the U.S. Senate on issues related to national security. Topics covered included nuclear deterrence, terrorist detainee policy, border security, Russia, Egypt, Afghanistan, Iraq and funding to Syrian rebel groups. The national security scorecard scores all Representatives and Senators on key national security votes in their respective chambers over the past two years. And while Congressman Carson claims *"As a former law enforcement officer with the Indiana Department of Homeland Security in the anti-terrorism unit, it is critical that Americans know that I would never associate with any individual or organization trying to harm the United States of America or its citizens,"*[193] he achieved only an abysmally low 11% on the CSP Congressional scorecard.

CONGRESSMAN CARSON'S FINANCIAL SUPPORT FROM THE MUSLIM BROTHERHOOD

Making matters even more serious for Congressman Carson, he has in fact been taking money from a number of self-identified Muslim Brotherhood front groups, including some that are members of the U.S. Muslim Brotherhood political party (the USCMO). The table in Appendix 1 includes political donations, as reported from 26 January 2008 through 26 October 2014 by the Federal Election Commission with a **total amount of**

---

[192] Center for Security Policy, "2013-2014 Congressional National Security Scorecard," 15 October 2014.
https://www.centerforsecuritypolicy.org/2014/10/15/2013-2014-national-security-scorecard/
[193] Congressman André Carson for the 7ᵗʰ District of Indiana, "Carson Statement on Attending the ICNA Chicago Convention," 31 December 2014.
http://carson.house.gov/media-center/press-releases/carson-statement-on-his-attendance-at-the-icna-chicago-convention

donations listed as $36,911.[194] In this chart, the "Confidence" level refers to the Islamist Watch certainty about names, name spellings, and correct identities.

It seems that André Carson wants to have it both ways: consort with the Brotherhood, take political donations from Brotherhood front groups, enjoy VIP status at Brotherhood events—and then try to cover his tracks by withholding transcripts and videos, issuing questionable media statements, and remaining mute as social media entries and other websites are scrubbed of information that might link him to events and groups and individuals now perhaps seen as too dubious even for André Carson.[195]

Congressman Keith Ellison has in fact been taking money from a number of self-identified Muslim Brotherhood front groups, including some that are members of the U.S. Muslim Brotherhood political party (the USCMO). The table in Appendix 2 includes political donations, as reported from 24 April 2006 through 3 November 2014 by the Federal Election Commission with a **total amount of donations listed as $136,092**.[196] In this chart, the "Confidence" level refers to the Islamist Watch certainty about names, name spellings, and correct identities.

---

[194] Islamist Watch, Islamist Money in Politics, Donations from Individuals Associated with American Islamist Groups, "Congressman Andre Carson," http://www.islamist-watch.org/money-politics/recipient/113/

[195] Center for Security Policy, "Center Releases Dossier Documenting a House Intelligence Committee Member's Extensive Ties to the Muslim Brotherhood,"24 February 2015. http://www.centerforsecuritypolicy.org/2015/02/24/center-releases-dossier-documenting-a-house-intelligence-committee-members-extensive-ties-to-the-muslim-brotherhood/

[196] Islamist Watch, Islamist Money in Politics, Donations from Individuals Associated with American Islamist Groups, "Congressman Keith Ellison," http://www.islamist-watch.org/money-politics/recipient/101/

SETTING SIGHTS ON 2016 AND BEYOND

While the Center's *Star Spangled Shariah: Rise of a Muslim Brotherhood Political Party* study spans nearly a year of in-depth analysis of the United States Council of Muslim Organizations (USCMO), this first U.S. political party openly associated with the jihadist Muslim Brotherhood is aggressively pursuing many of its operational objectives behind closed doors. Some of its public activities, such as the 13 April 2015 "Advocacy Day on Capitol Hill," clearly were programmed with an eye on the 2016 presidential election cycle. But others, such as the concluding remarks by USCMO Secretary General Oussama Jammal when he addressed thousands of Muslim Brotherhood supporters about future USCMO plans near the end of the 13th annual Muslim American Society-Islamic Circle of North America (MAS-ICNA) convention at the McCormick Place in Chicago on 28 December 2014, still have not been made available to the American public. Nor has a full electronic record or transcripts for speeches given by current Congressmen André Carson and Keith Ellison during the USCMO's June 2014 inaugural banquet ever been published.

Concern is warranted first and foremost because the USCMO, given its member groups' affiliation with the openly jihadist Muslim Brotherhood, threatens U.S. national security and takes aim at the U.S. Constitution. Muslim Brotherhood plans long in law enforcement possession describe a stealthy process of infiltration and subversion that many Americans, including among top levels of the nation's security agencies, nevertheless are ill-prepared to recognize or counter. And in just one year of operation, the USCMO has shown itself a stealthy operator whose leadership carefully manages its online presence and conceals what it is not willing to share with the American people who are its target.

Since the USCMO's inception in March 2014, the organization more than once has relied upon a less-than-transparent modus operandi that obscures its true agenda, activities, and intentions for the U.S. political process from the general public and even members of Congress. A strong commitment to development of the next generation of American Muslim Brotherhood leadership, however, stands out as one of its more evident objectives, as the USCMO's mentoring of young people and special event programs geared to youth demonstrate. But it is the Brotherhood's—and therefore, the USCMO's—dedication to establishing a Shariah-adherent agenda for the U.S. that marks its development as a religious identity political party with particular concern. That its Muslim Brotherhood affiliations bring with them a hostility to the U.S. Constitution and its established liberties (because they derive from man-made law) as well as a track record of conducting sophisticated influence operations against U.S. law enforcement and intelligence agencies only underlines the security threat from this new grouping.

Troubling examples that seem to underscore the USCMO's stealth jihad agenda dotted its first year. As noted above, Congressmen Carson and Ellison, who are financially supported by known Muslim Brotherhood front organizations, have not responded to public requests to either make available the transcripts of their speeches or to explain why they were in fact participating at a USCMO event in an official capacity. Following the still-shrouded proceedings of its inaugural banquet, the USCMO participated in anti-Semitic, pro-HAMAS and pro-Muslim Brotherhood demonstrations and raised funds for Islamic Relief USA, a large U.S. Muslim charity with its own dubious record. The USCMO debuted in Illinois politics during the midterm 2014 election cycle, led by Sabri Samirah, a veteran Jordanian Muslim Brotherhood leader who was banned from entering the U.S. for a decade because he was deemed a national security risk. As information became public regarding Samirah's return to the U.S. and his work with the USCMO, he made a number of rather clumsy online attempts to erase and otherwise conceal such activities.

As the USCMO developed its plans heading into the 2016 presidential election cycle for mobilizing its base across the country in "get out the vote" efforts to influence key elections, events unfolding in Egypt as well as Washington, D.C. provided a glimpse of the linkages that bind it to its parent organization, the Egyptian Muslim Brotherhood. Egyptian President Abdel Fatah al-Sisi's ongoing struggle to suppress the Brotherhood coincided starkly with early 2015 high level meetings involving Muslim Brotherhood leadership figures held in Washington, D.C. with the U.S. Department of State and White House.

STATE DEPARTMENT AND WHITE HOUSE MEETINGS WITH MUSLIM BROTHERHOOD LEADERSHIP

On 27 January 2015, the U.S. Department of State hosted[197] a delegation of Muslim Brotherhood-aligned leaders. In attendance was Waleed Sharaby, secretary-general of the Egyptian Revolutionary Council and a spokesman for the group Judges for Egypt. In his picture taken at the State Department, Sharaby boldly flashed the Muslim Brotherhood's notorious four-finger Rabia hand sign. Accompanying Sharaby on his WDC trip was Gamal Heshmat, a leading member of the Brotherhood, and Abdel Mawgoud al-Dardery, a Brotherhood parliamentary member from Luxor, Egypt. While the State Department declined to provide anything substantive regarding the talks, parties in attendance, or the U.S. government hosts, the delegation's visit seemed to set the stage for a closed-door meeting that U.S. President Barack Obama subsequently held with high level U.S. Muslim Brotherhood leadership figures on 4 February 2015.

President Obama met[198] with key leadership from Muslim Brotherhood, including the Islamic Society of North America (ISNA) President Azhar Azeez[199] and Imam Mohamed Magid[200], the current President of the All Dulles Area Muslim Society (ADAMS) Center, an Obama-appointed[201] adviser to DHS in 2011, and past president of ISNA. Obama would surely have known as he met with Magid and Azeez, that ISNA was named an unindicted co-conspirator by the Department of Justice in the 2008 Holy Land Foundation HAMAS terror funding trial, which sent its leadership to jail and shut down the so-called charity group. Incidentally, Azeez just happens to be the National Director of Islamic Relief USA, a group which USCMO members assisted in fundraising efforts

[197] Adam Kredo, "Muslim Brotherhood-Aligned Leaders Hosted at State Department: Brotherhood seeks to rally anti-Sisi support," *The Washington Free Beacon*, 28 January 2015. http://freebeacon.com/national-security/muslim-brotherhood-leaders-hosted-at-state-department/

[198] IBD Editorials, "Obama Invited Leader Of Terror Co-Conspirator Group To Meeting," *Investor's Business Daily*, 6 February 2015. http://news.investors.com/ibd-editorials/020615-738417-secret-white-house-meeting-included-known-jihadist-group-members.htm

[199] Islamic Society of North America, "ISNA President: Azhar Azeez," http://www.isna.net/azhar-azeez.html, accessed 24 February 2015

[200] Discover the Networks, "Islamic Society of North America," http://www.discoverthenetworks.org/individualProfile.asp?indid=2562

[201] John Rossomando, The Investigative Project on Terrorism, "Egyptian Magazine: Muslim Brotherhood Infiltrates Obama Administration," 3 January 2013. http://www.investigativeproject.org/3869/egyptian-magazine-muslim-brotherhood-infiltrates

in September 2014 in Chicago. It is important to note that Azeez also is President of the North Texas Islamic Council, and a founding member & past President of the Council on American Islamic Relations in Dallas[202], and President of the Islamic Association of Carrollton, Texas, one of the large mosques in the Dallas, TX suburbs.

Islamic Society of North America's Connections to the USCMO

While ISNA is not listed as an official member of the USCMO, under the leadership of Azeez, the North Texas Islamic Council works closely with the USCMO member organization, the Muslim Legal Fund of America, directed by J. Khalil Meek. Significantly, a colleague of Azeez is Mohamed Elibiary[203], also a cofounder of the North Texas Islamic Council, and past CAIR Dallas-Fort Worth board member. Elibiary was appointed by the Obama administration in 2010 to serve on the U.S. Department of Homeland Security's Countering Violent Extremism Working Group (CVEWG) and the DHS Faith-Based Security and Communications Advisory Committee. Elibiary's earlier association with DHS and working knowledge of the CVEWG likely would offer valuable insights for the USCMO. Influence also has flowed in the other direction as well. Beginning in late 2011, in response[204] to pressure from Magid[205] and other Muslim Brotherhood-linked operators such as Salam al-Marayati, the President of the Muslim Public Affairs Council (MPAC), a U.S. government-wide purge removed all training curriculum materials that would portray accurately the inspirational role of Islamic doctrine, law, and scripture for acts of Islamic terrorism. The Federal Bureau of Investigation alone purged[206] some 700 documents and 300 presentations from its training materials and lesson plans in 2012. Magid also served as a member[207] on the FBI's Sikh, Muslim, and

[202] CAIR Texas, DFW Chapter, "Speakers: Azhar Azeez," http://www.cair-dfw.org/speakers/aazeez.htm, accessed 9 February 2015

[203] Discover the Networks, "Mohamed Elibiary," http://www.discoverthenetworks.org/individualProfile.asp?indid=2560

[204] Clare Lopez, Counter Jihad Report, "Jihads Willing Executioners," 5 June 2012. http://counterjihadreport.com/2012/06/05/jihads-willing-executioners/

[205] Jordan Schachtel, Counter Jihad Report, "NYT Profiles 'Counter Extremists' Who Are Actually Extremists," 22 February 2015. http://counterjihadreport.com/2015/02/22/nyt-profiles-counter-extremists-who-are-actually-extremists/

[206] Omar Sacirbey, "FBI, Muslims report progress over training materials," *Washington Post*, 16 February 2012. http://www.washingtonpost.com/national/on-faith/fbi-muslims-report-progress-over-training-materials/2012/02/16/gIQA7R7KIR_story.html

[207] Discover the Networks, "Mohamed Magid," http://www.discoverthenetworks.org/individualProfile.asp?indid=2562

Arab Advisory Board. Thus, the careful groundwork established by the Muslim Brotherhood eventually paved the way for the USCMO.

USCMO LEADERSHIP MEET WITH U.S. DEPARTMENT OF HOMELAND SECURITY OFFICIALS

In the summer of 2014, USCMO leadership met with U.S. Department of Homeland Security officials. Topics covered included civil rights and countering so-called 'violent extremism.' As reported[208] by the USCMO on 5 August 2014, "The delegations also discussed future cooperation between the Council members and DHS with a focus on increasing engagements on a local level." The USCMO leadership delegation included Secretary General Oussama Jammal; Nihad Awad and Robert McCaw of the Council on American-Islamic Relations (CAIR); Naeem Baig and Rameez Abed of the Islamic Circle of North America (ICNA); Osama Abu Irshaid of the American Muslims for Palestine (AMP) and Imam Talib Shareef of The Mosque Cares-Ministry of Imam W.D. Mohammed. The divisions from DHS that were represented included following: the Civil Rights and Civil Liberty (CRCL); Countering Violent Extremism (CVE); Counterterrorism; TSA; the Homeland Security Advisory Council and the Faith-based Security and Communications Advisory Subcommittee (FBAC).

USCMO leadership meet with US DHS officials

---

[208] US Council of Muslim Organizations, "USCMO Leadership Meet With DHS Officials," 5 August 2014. http://www.uscmo.org/councilnews/, accessed 27 January 2015

This meeting evidently established the parameters for the USCMO to plan a 10 February 2015 "Community Forum on Countering Violent Extremism," in Washington, DC that was sponsored by the Zakat Foundation of America. The USCMO event took place one week in advance of the Obama administration's own widely-touted CVE summit to address "violent extremism," held 18 February 2015.

In the early lead-up to the U.S. 2016 presidential election, the USCMO and Secretary General Oussama Jammal organized an unprecedented "First National Muslim Advocacy Day on Capitol Hill" for 13 April 2015. The first U.S. Muslim Brotherhood political party described[209] this advocacy day on its website as "one of the next steps in growing the American Muslim community's political capacity and ability to "move the needle" in Washington, D.C." In view of just how far Muslim Brotherhood influence operations already have succeeded in "moving the needle" of U.S. foreign and domestic policy on critical issues involving Islamic terror and the Muslim Brotherhood, the continued development of the USCMO as a U.S. political movement requires close attention from both citizens and legislators. Sophisticated operations directed by the Muslim Brotherhood and cloaked in red, white, and blue but fixed steadfastly on the advancement of Shariah in America must be recognized as the "Star Spangled Shariah" deception they are.

---

[209] US Council of Muslim Organizations, "National Advocacy Day," http://www.uscmo.org/national-advocacy-day/, accessed 28 January 2015

USCMO Secretary General Oussama Jammal introducing USCMO leadership at 13ᵗʰ Annual MAS-ICNA Convention on December 28, 2014

MORAL RESPONSIBILITY OF UNITED STATES CITIZENS: SELF-EDUCATION & CIVIC ENGAGEMENT

The United States of America faces a clear and present danger from the Muslim Brotherhood through the United States Council of Muslim Organizations members because of their Shariah compliant agenda that supports and advocates jihad. Both in contravention of and hostile to the United States Constitution, the supremacist, totalitarian aspects of Shariah are incompatible with our Republic and natural law. The USCMO's "Star Spangled Shariah" narrative, combined with an agenda to manipulate the U.S. political system and co-opt disaffected non-Muslim segments of society to advance the Muslim Brotherhood's Civilization Jihad requires immediate action by citizens, faith leadership, the law enforcement community, and legislators.

Ronald Reagan, the 40ᵗʰ President of the U.S., once stated: "Freedom is never more than one generation away from extinction. We didn't pass it to our children in the bloodstream. It must be fought for, protected, and handed on for them to do the same, or one day we will spend our sunset years telling our children and our children's children what it was once like in the United States where men were free." In order to preserve and protect this freedom, the following areas represent actionable items that must be taken by citizens in this country:

* Understand the difference between Shariah and the U.S. Constitution http://www.centerforsecuritypolicy.org/upload/wysiwyg/article%20pdfs/Shariah_VS_Constitution.pdf;
* Join fellow citizens to advance the passage of American Laws for American Courts legislation in your state http://www.centerforsecuritypolicy.org/tag/american-laws-for-american-courts/;
* Educate and meet with elected representatives when they are in their home district or in Washington, D.C. and urge them to investigate the "Star Spangled Shariah" activities and influence operations of the Muslim Brotherhood in your community;
* Object publicly the conversion of churches into mosques, such as the First Assembly of God in Wheaton, Illinois taken over by the USCMO member Islamic Center of Wheaton in December 2013;
* Engage in the electoral process, question candidates publicly about Islam and Shariah, and volunteer for campaigns with like-minded candidates at local, state, and federal level;
* Monitor interfaith religious dialogue meetings in your community where Muslim Brotherhood front organizations and/or USCMO members have an active role;
* Utilize social media tools to present facts to the public about the duplicitous modus operandi of the Muslim Brotherhood and its Civilization Jihad strategy in the United States;
* Follow the Center for Security Policy for updates about the ongoing USCMO activities, send letters to editors of papers, and use a blog site to share this information with concerned citizens; and
* Invite subject matter experts from the Center for Security Policy to speak at churches, synagogues, patriotic groups, or other venues in your community.

APPENDIX 1: THE MUSLIM BROTHERHOOD AND HOSTILE INTELLIGENCE GATHERING

According to documents acquired by Federal and foreign law enforcement agencies, the Muslim Brotherhood has instructed its members to engage in hostile intelligence gathering and influence operations against the United States.

One such document is the December 1982 document discovered by Swiss law enforcement in the Lugano, Switzerland home of self-identified Muslim Brotherhood financier Yousef Nada.[210]

MB/HAMAS member Azzam Tamimi identified that the document, known as the "Global Project for Palestine" (and often called, simply, "The Project") had been prepared by the MB in Amman, Jordan.[211] The document instructs the MB to establish intelligence capabilities:

THE TENTH POINT OF DEPARTURE

To use diverse and varied surveillance systems, in several places, to gather information and adopt a single effective warning system serving the worldwide Islamic movement. In fact, surveillance, policy decisions and effective communications complement each other.

a-Elements:
To make the policy decisions to collect important and precise information.
To diffuse Islamic policy so that it is largely and efficiently covered by the media.

---

[210] For the text of the Project see, The Investigative Project on Terrorism, "The Project," http://www.investigativeproject.org/documents/misc/687.pdf. Nada's authorized biography is entitled, "Inside the Muslim Brotherhood: The Truth About the World's Most Powerful Political Movement," http://www.amazon.com/Inside-Muslim-Brotherhood-Powerful-Political/dp/1857826876 For more on The Project and its discovery by Swiss law enforcement see, Patrick Poole, "The Muslim Brotherhood "Project", Frontpage Magazine, May 11, 2006, http://archive.frontpagemag.com/readarticle.aspx?ARTID=4476

[211] Patrick Poole, "The Origins of the Muslim Brotherhood 'Project'" FrontPage Magazine, July 24, 2008 http://archive.frontpagemag.com/readarticle.aspx?ARTID=4476

b-Procedures:
To create a modern surveillance system by means of advanced technology (possibly created at the research centers mentioned earlier). To create an effective and serious media centre.

c- Suggested Missions:
To warn Muslims of the dangers that threaten them and the international conspiracies directed at them.
To give our views on current events and future issues.

The document also instructs the MB to conduct influence operations targeting "Centers of power" worldwide:

THE FIFTH POINT OF DEPARTURE

To dedicate ourselves to the establishment of an Islamic state, in parallel with gradual efforts aimed at gaining control of local power centers through institutional action.

a- Elements
To channel thought, education and action in order to establish an Islamic power [government] on the earth.
To influence centers of power both local and worldwide to the service of Islam.

b- Procedures
To prepare a scientific study on the possibility of establishing the reign of God throughout the world according to established priorities.
To study the centers of power, both local and worldwide, and the possibilities of placing them under influence.
To conduct a modern study on the concept of support for the *dawa* and Islamic law, and more particularly on the men of influence in the State and the country.

While the "Project" document appears to provide only vague guidelines for future effort, the Charter of the Center of the Studies, the Intelligence and the Information, uncovered in a search of the home of convicted Palestinian Islamic Jihad organizer Sami Al-Arian, was described by Federal Agent David Kane in an affidavit as "a comprehensive plan to establish a hostile intelligence organization in the United States and elsewhere."[212] Included in the Charter are specific instructions to target U.S. intelligence-gathering agencies. In the Affidavit Kane writes regarding the Charter:

> 43. Also located at the search of Al-Arian's residence was a document, hand written in Arabic, called the Charter of the Center of the Studies, the Intelligence and the Information. This document, hereinafter called "the Charter," set forth a comprehensive plan to establish a hostile intelligence organization in the United States and elsewhere. It stated that:
>> Our presence in North America gives us a unique opportunity to monitor, explore and follow up . . . . We are in the center which leads the conspiracy against our Islamic world . . . . Therefore, we, here can monitor and watch the American policies and the activities of those questionable organizations . . . . Therefore, we have the capability to establish a Center for Studies, Intelligence and Information.
>
> 44. The Charter provided for a "Division of Security and Military Affairs," whose functions were to
>> prepare training programs for the brothers. These programs include physical training, surveillance training . . . programs for military training benefitting from the available opportunities that exist in this country . . . . To make technical studies with the objective of availing spying and military tools and devices to the Group in America and the East and about the spying methods and equipment in these countries.
>
> 45. The Charter provided for an Organization/Law Studies Section whose job it would be to study the legal aspect of establishing charitable organizations in America.
>
> 46. The Charter provided for the establishment of an Intelligence and Monitoring Apparatus, part of which would be responsible to "to watch the individuals who oppose the Movement and the Islamic actions. To watch them, monitor them and to make files on them. . . 30 ." Members of the Group should be able to "infiltrate the sensitive intelligence agencies or the embassies in order to collect information and build close relationships with the people in charge in these establishments." They should also use every opportunity to "collect information from those relatives and friends who work in sensitive positions in the government, et cetera . . . ."

The MB's record of creating intelligence organs and engage in hostile intelligence operations has also been noted in the press. A February,

---

[212] David Kane, "AFFIDAVIT IN SUPPORT OF APPLICATION FOR SEARCH WARRANT", OCTOBER 2003 accessed https://www.investigativeproject.org/documents/case_docs/891.pdf The entire Charter can be read at http://www.investigativeproject.org/documents/case_docs/533.pdf

21, 2011 Associated Press article noted that, "[MB deputy guide Khairat] el-Shater, according to the former Brotherhood members and security officials, is suspected of running an information gathering operation capable of eavesdropping on telephones and email." Additionally the report noted former members as indicating "the group had six "mini intelligence centers," including one housed in its headquarters in the Cairo district of Moqqatam."[213]

Additionally, individuals with identified connections to Foreign Intelligence Services (FIS) have been noted to have MB connections. For example, there is the case of Ghulam Nabi Fai, an individual who pled guilty to serving as an unregistered Foreign Agent for Pakistan's ISIS intelligence service.[214] Fai served on the Advisory Council of ISNA and had numerous other MB connections.[215] Fai and Rep. Carson both were speakers at the 39th Annual ICNA-MAS convention, although they did not appear on the same panels.[216]

[213] Associated Press, "Egypt's Brotherhood still operates secretively," February 21, 2013 http://www.ynetnews.com/articles/0,7340,L-4347738,00.html

[214] Patrick Poole, "The Biggest D.C. Spy Scandal You Haven't Heard About (Part One)," August 14, 2012, PJ Media, http://pjmedia.com/blog/the-biggest-d-c-spy-scandal-you-havent-heard-about-part-one/?singlepage=true

[215] Patrick Poole, "The Biggest D.C. Spy Scandal You Haven't Heard About (Part Two)" PJ Media, August 16, 2012, http://pjmedia.com/blog/the-biggest-d-c-spy-scandal-you-havent-heard-about-part-two/?singlepage=true

[216] For confirmation that Fai attended 39th annual ICNA-Mas Conference see: "Modi – Sharif Meeting Offers Hope for Peace In South Asia: Dr. Fai", KashmirWatch.com, May 28, 2014, http://kashmirwatch.com/index.php/2014/05/28/modi-8211-sharif-meeting-offers-hope-for-peace-in-south-asia-dr-fai.html

APPENDIX 2: MUSLIM BROTHERHOOD FINANCING CONGRESSMAN ANDRÉ CARSON

Islamist Money in Politics: Donations from Individuals Associated with American Islamist Groups[217]

Date	Name	Affiliation	Amount
2014-10-26	Hisham Abdallah	MAS	$750
2014-09-20	Mohammad Jadid	CAIR	$500
2014-09-20	Samir Mokaddem	CAIR	$250
2014-09-14	Nayyer Ali	MPAC	$1000
2014-06-30	Hashem Mubarak	CAIR	$2500
2014-05-23	Ashraf Sufi	ISNA	$500
2014-04-25	Amir Khaliq	CAIR	$1000
2014-03-30	Mohammad Yunus	ICNA	$2000
2014-03-29	Mohammad Yunus	ICNA	$500
2014-02-17	Shariq Siddiqui	ISNA	$250
2013-12-10	Ahmed Bedier	CAIR	$250
2013-12-07	Muhammad Saleem	CAIR	$250
2013-11-17	Kamal Yassin	CAIR	$1000
2013-11-17	Anjum Shariff	CAIR	$500
2013-04-17	Athar Siddiqee	CAIR	$500
2013-04-13	Manzoor Ghori	ISNA	$250
2012-10-19	Muhammad Saleem	CAIR	$300

[217] Islamist Watch, Islamist Money in Politics, Donations from Individuals Associated with American Islamist Groups, "Congressman Andre Carson," http://www.islamist-watch.org/money-politics/recipient/113/

2012-09-13	Nayyer Ali	MPAC	$1000
2012-09-10	Asad Malik	CAIR	$500
2012-08-28	Tahra Goraya	CAIR	$250
2012-06-30	Rashid Abbara	CAIR	$700
2012-04-25	Shaukat Gaziani	CAIR	$250
2012-04-21	Safdar Khwaja	CAIR	$300
2012-04-21	Azmat Qayyum	CAIR	$200
2012-04-21	Azmat Qayyum	CAIR	$500
2012-04-15	Azhar Azeez	ISNA, CAIR	$1035
2012-04-14	Azhar Azeez	ISNA, CAIR	$1000
2011-12-04	Azeez Farooki	MPAC	$1000
2011-09-30	Dalia Mahmoud	MPAC	$500
2011-03-28	Muzammil Ahmed	CAIR	$1000
2010-09-30	Nayyer Ali	MPAC	$2400
2010-09-10	Muzammil Ahmed	CAIR	$500
2010-08-01	Dalia Mahmoud	MPAC	$1000
2010-07-23	Azeez Farooki	MPAC	$300
2009-12-27	Haris Tarin	MPAC	$300
2009-11-01	Rizwan Jaka	ISNA, CAIR	$250
2009-07-23	Dalia Mahmoud	MPAC	$500
2009-07-12	Malik Sarwar	MPAC, CAIR	$350
2009-02-27	Dalia Mahmoud	MPAC	$230
2009-02-27	Dalia Mahmoud	MPAC	$500
2008-12-12	Khurrum Wahid	CAIR	$250
2008-12-12	Khurrum Wahid	CAIR	$400

2008-11-03	Asad Malik	CAIR	$250
2008-09-30	Dalia Mahmoud	MPAC	$1000
2008-09-07	Anbar Mahar	CAIR	$250
2008-05-01	Rizwan Jaka	ISNA, CAIR	$300
2008-04-22	Khurrum Wahid	CAIR	$716
2008-04-22	Rashid Abbara	CAIR	$1500
2008-04-22	Suhail Nanji	CAIR	$1000
2008-04-22	Ahmed Al Shehab	CAIR	$250
2008-04-22	Asad Ba-Yunus	ISNA	$250
2008-04-22	Asad Ba-Yunus	ISNA	$250
2008-03-03	Rashid Abbara	CAIR	$500
2008-03-03	Esam Omeish	CAIR, MAS	$500
2008-02-10	Tahra Goraya	CAIR	$250
2008-02-08	Rizwan Jaka	ISNA, CAIR	$300
2008-01-29	Shahid Athar	ISNA	$1000
2008-01-29	M. Affan Badar	ISNA	$250
2008-01-26	Shariq Siddiqui	ISNA	$330
2008-01-26	Shariq Siddiqui	ISNA	$500

TOTAL = **$36,911**

APPENDIX 3: MUSLIM BROTHERHOOD FINANCING CONGRESSMAN KEITH ELLISON

Islamist Money in Politics: Donations from Individuals Associated with American Islamist Groups [218]

Date	Name	Affiliation	Amount
2014-11-03	Kashif Saroya	CAIR	$1000
2014-09-14	Nayyer Ali	MPAC	$1000
2014-09-08	Hussam Ayloush	CAIR	$200
2014-08-29	Malik Sarwar	MPAC, CAIR	$500
2014-08-12	Hassan Ahmad	CAIR	$500
2014-07-22	Erfan Obeid	CAIR	$250
2014-06-12	Muzammil Ahmed	CAIR	$500
2014-06-08	Dalia Mahmoud	MPAC	$400
2014-06-08	Dalia Mahmoud	MPAC	$1600
2014-03-14	Hashem Mubarak	CAIR	$250
2014-02-07	Ayman Hammous	MAS	$250
2014-02-06	Hassan Ahmad	CAIR	$500
2014-01-27	Hassan Ahmad	CAIR	$400
2013-12-31	Tarek Hussein	CAIR	$1000
2013-12-31	Junaid Malik	CAIR	$250
2013-12-27	Hashem Mubarak	CAIR	$250
2013-11-21	Amir Khaliq	CAIR	$750

---

[218] Islamist Watch, Islamist Money in Politics, Donations from Individuals Associated with American Islamist Groups, "Congressman Keith Ellison," http://www.islamist-watch.org/money-politics/recipient/101/

2013-11-17	Ahmed Bedier	CAIR	$1000
2013-10-24	Muzammil Ahmed	CAIR	$1000
2013-10-21	Yahya Basha	MPAC	$500
2013-10-10	Esam Omeish	CAIR, MAS	$500
2013-09-30	Junaid Malik	CAIR	$250
2013-09-26	Hashem Mubarak	CAIR	$250
2013-09-23	Noor Zubeida Khan	MPAC	$300
2013-09-17	Nayyer Ali	MPAC	$2500
2013-09-13	Mazen Kudaimi	CAIR	$1000
2013-09-11	Hadia Mubarak	ISNA, CAIR	$250
2013-09-11	Akram Elzend	MAS	$1000
2013-08-05	Zead Ramadan	CAIR	$500
2013-07-19	Akram Elzend	MAS	$500
2013-06-24	Suhail Nanji	CAIR	$500
2013-05-13	Asad Zaman	MAS	$250
2013-03-18	Basim Elkarra	CAIR	$251
2013-03-15	Rashid Ahmad	CAIR	$250
2013-03-12	Fawzia Keval	CAIR	$250
2013-03-12	Jeffrey Saladin	CAIR	$250
2013-01-17	James (Khalil) Meek	CAIR	$1000
2012-12-11	Dalia Mahmoud	MPAC	$1000
2012-11-04	Hashem Mubarak	CAIR	$250
2012-09-30	Shafath Syed	CAIR	$500
2012-09-27	Khalique Zahir	ISNA	$500
2012-09-21	Ashraf Sufi	ISNA	$1000
2012-09-17	Hashem Mubarak	CAIR	$250

2012-09-13	Nayyer Ali	MPAC	$1000
2012-09-01	Hashem Mubarak	CAIR	$250
2012-08-14	Naveen Bhora	MPAC	$500
2012-08-13	Rizwan Jaka	ISNA, CAIR	$250
2012-08-10	Khurrum Wahid	CAIR	$250
2012-08-08	Asad Zaman	MAS	$250
2012-07-25	Mudusar Raza	CAIR	$200
2012-07-16	Yahya Basha	MPAC	$400
2012-06-24	Atif Fareed	CAIR	$250
2012-06-12	Mohammed Saleem	CAIR	$400
2012-06-10	Jawad Shah	ISNA	$1000
2012-06-01	Hashem Mubarak	CAIR	$250
2012-05-15	Mohammed Saleem	CAIR	$200
2012-05-15	Thasin Sardar	CAIR	$250
2012-04-14	Khurrum Wahid	CAIR	$500
2012-03-30	Nasir Mahmood	CAIR	$250
2012-03-28	Zead Ramadan	CAIR	$1000
2012-03-12	Azeez Farooki	MPAC	$500
2012-03-07	Dalia Mahmoud	MPAC	$1000
2012-01-28	Ahmed Younis	MPAC	$250
2011-12-20	Khurrum Wahid	CAIR	$300
2011-12-19	Rashid Abbara	CAIR	$500
2011-12-19	Suhail Nanji	CAIR	$1000
2011-12-05	Ahmed Al Shehab	CAIR	$300
2011-12-05	Samih Abbassi	CAIR	$500

2011-11-30	Muzammil Ahmed	CAIR	$1000
2011-11-07	Kenneth Gamble	MANA	$1000
2011-11-07	Iftekhar Hussain	CAIR	$375
2011-10-27	Zead Ramadan	CAIR	$300
2011-06-01	Shamel Abd-Allah	CAIR	$500
2011-05-31	Yaser Tabbara	CAIR	$500
2011-05-07	Asad Zaman	MAS	$200
2011-03-31	Ashraf Sufi	ISNA	$500
2011-03-21	Mohammed Saleem	CAIR	$500
2011-03-21	Jawad Shah	ISNA	$2000
2011-03-17	Yahya Basha	MPAC	$500
2011-03-16	Asad Malik	CAIR	$500
2011-03-16	Haaris Ahmad	CAIR	$2400
2011-02-15	Dalia Mahmoud	MPAC	$1000
2011-01-26	Naveen Bhora	MPAC	$500
2011-01-26	Shafath Syed	CAIR	$250
2010-11-01	Dalia Mahmoud	MPAC	$1100
2010-10-19	Rizwan Jaka	ISNA, CAIR	$300
2010-10-11	Esam Omeish	CAIR, MAS	$250
2010-09-27	Nayyer Ali	MPAC	$2400
2010-06-30	Dalia Mahmoud	MPAC	$200
2010-06-30	Dalia Mahmoud	MPAC	$1300
2010-06-30	Azeez Farooki	MPAC	$500
2010-06-30	Safaa Zarzour	ISNA, CAIR	$-500
2010-06-29	Zead Ramadan	CAIR	$400

2010-06-29	Zead Ramadan	CAIR	$600
2010-06-29	Suzanne Akhras Sahloul	CAIR	$500
2010-06-11	Rashid Abbara	CAIR	$1000
2010-06-10	Asad Zaman	MAS	$500
2010-05-24	Safaa Zarzour	ISNA, CAIR	$500
2010-05-24	Mazen Kudaimi	CAIR	$2000
2010-05-24	Ahmed Rehab	CAIR	$250
2010-05-24	Emad Hamwi	CAIR	$200
2010-05-18	Zaid Abdur-Rahman	CAIR	$300
2010-05-12	Dalia Mahmoud	MPAC	$500
2010-04-21	Dalia Mahmoud	MPAC	$1000
2010-04-13	Emad Hamwi	CAIR	$300
2010-03-26	Esam Omeish	CAIR, MAS	$500
2010-03-24	Zead Ramadan	CAIR	$250
2010-03-24	Zead Ramadan	CAIR	$500
2010-01-26	Asad Zaman	MAS	$250
2009-12-14	Safaa Zarzour	ISNA, CAIR	$250
2009-09-28	Zead Ramadan	CAIR	$250
2009-09-21	Mannan Mohammed	CAIR	$500
2009-09-21	Mohamed El-Sharkawy	CAIR	$500
2009-09-14	Suhail Nanji	CAIR	$1000
2009-07-21	Dalia Mahmoud	MPAC	$700
2009-07-21	Zead Ramadan	CAIR	$1000
2009-07-21	Wael Hamza	MAS	$250
2009-07-09	Asad Malik	CAIR	$250

2009-06-17	Esam Omeish	CAIR, MAS	$500
2009-06-15	Magdy Eletreby	MPAC	$500
2009-06-13	Rizwan Jaka	ISNA, CAIR	$250
2009-03-16	Yahya Basha	MPAC	$500
2009-03-16	Muzammil Ahmed	CAIR	$500
2009-02-28	Owais Siddiqui	CAIR	$500
2008-11-17	Atif Fareed	CAIR	$500
2008-11-17	Mohamed Ghabour	CAIR	$500
2008-10-31	Yahya Basha	MPAC	$300
2008-10-20	Fouad Khatib	CAIR	$200
2008-10-20	Shafath Syed	CAIR	$500
2008-10-20	Safaa Ibrahim	CAIR	$300
2008-10-20	Razi Mohiuddin	CAIR	$1000
2008-09-29	Zead Ramadan	CAIR	$1000
2008-09-19	Esam Omeish	CAIR, MAS	$500
2008-09-08	Tarek Hussein	CAIR	$500
2008-09-08	Tarek Hussein	CAIR	$500
2008-09-02	Mohammed Alo	CAIR	$250
2008-08-19	Hesham Hassaballa	CAIR	$500
2008-08-19	Suzanne Akhras Sahloul	CAIR	$1000
2008-08-06	Jawad Shah	ISNA	$2300
2008-08-04	Haaris Ahmad	CAIR	$312
2008-07-31	Haaris Ahmad	CAIR	$205
2008-07-31	Muzammil Ahmed	CAIR	$1000
2008-07-28	Asad Malik	CAIR	$1000

2008-07-28	Jukaku Tayeb	CAIR	$1000
2008-07-11	Dalia Mahmoud	MPAC	$500
2008-05-19	Asad Zaman	MAS	$300
2008-04-14	Karen Dabdoub	CAIR	$250
2008-04-07	Mazen Kudaimi	CAIR	$1000
2008-03-15	Malik Sarwar	MPAC, CAIR	$1000
2008-03-14	Zead Ramadan	CAIR	$1200
2008-03-11	Dalia Mahmoud	MPAC	$500
2008-03-11	Aliya Latif	CAIR	$400
2008-03-01	Rizwan Jaka	ISNA, CAIR	$500
2008-02-18	Hyder Ali	CAIR	$1000
2008-02-18	Hany Elkordy	CAIR	$250
2008-02-18	James Yee	CAIR	$500
2008-02-01	Magdy Eletreby	MPAC	$2300
2007-12-05	Tahra Goraya	CAIR	$250
2007-12-02	Rashid Abbara	CAIR	$2000
2007-12-02	Syed Ali Rahman	CAIR	$300
2007-12-02	Suhail Nanji	CAIR	$500
2007-12-02	Asad Ba-Yunus	ISNA	$250
2007-12-01	Atif Fareed	CAIR	$2300
2007-12-01	Mohamed Ghabour	CAIR	$2300
2007-12-01	Raza Ali	CAIR	$250
2007-11-30	Parvez Ahmed	CAIR	$500
2007-11-21	Esam Omeish	CAIR, MAS	$450
2007-11-12	Nayyer Ali	MPAC	$2300

2007-09-04	Muzammil Ahmed	CAIR	$400
2007-08-27	Mohammad Jadid	CAIR	$250
2007-08-27	Samir Mokaddem	CAIR	$300
2007-07-25	Athar Siddiqee	CAIR	$1000
2007-07-24	Fouad Khatib	CAIR	$250
2007-07-24	Khaldoon Abugharbieh	CAIR	$250
2007-07-24	Razi Mohiuddin	CAIR	$2000
2007-06-30	Sherif Gindy	CAIR	$250
2007-06-30	Muzammil Ahmed	CAIR	$250
2007-05-04	Azhar Azeez	ISNA, CAIR	$500
2007-05-04	Ghulam Warriach	CAIR	$300
2007-05-04	Shaukat Gaziani	CAIR	$250
2007-04-20	Mazen Kudaimi	CAIR	$1000
2007-03-30	Yahya Basha	MPAC	$500
2007-01-08	Esam Omeish	CAIR, MAS	$1000
2007-01-08	Muhamad Albadawi	MAS	$1000
2006-10-31	Muhammad Saleem	CAIR	$250
2006-10-29	Shafath Syed	CAIR	$250
2006-10-29	Razi Mohiuddin	CAIR	$2000
2006-10-29	Manzoor Ghori	ISNA	$500
2006-10-28	Rizwan Jaka	ISNA, CAIR	$250
2006-10-23	Sherif Gindy	CAIR	$300
2006-10-23	Jukaku Tayeb	CAIR	$500
2006-10-23	Yahya Basha	MPAC	$500
2006-10-19	Asad Zaman	MAS	$400

2006-10-17	Parvez Ahmed	CAIR	$250
2006-10-16	Atif Fareed	CAIR	$2100
2006-10-16	Ezzat Zaki	CAIR	$1000
2006-10-16	Mohamed Ghabour	CAIR	$500
2006-10-16	Mohamed Ghabour	CAIR	$1500
2006-10-16	Raza Ali	CAIR	$250
2006-10-16	Suhail Nanji	CAIR	$1000
2006-09-24	Yahya Basha	MPAC	$300
2006-09-12	Hyder Ali	CAIR	$1000
2006-08-29	Esam Omeish	CAIR, MAS	$500
2006-08-28	James Yee	CAIR	$1000
2006-08-23	Mohamed Ghabour	CAIR	$999
2006-08-19	Asad Zaman	MAS	$1000
2006-08-11	Ghulam Warriach	CAIR	$250
2006-08-07	Parvez Ahmed	CAIR	$250
2006-07-25	Parvez Ahmed	CAIR	$250
2006-07-23	Corey Saylor	CAIR	$1000
2006-07-22	Nihad Awad	CAIR	$2000
2006-04-24	Esam Omeish	CAIR, MAS	$500

TOTAL = **$136,092**